A WEALDEN VILLAGE: MARDEN

To the History Group,
in celebration and with thanks for all the help and encouragement which made
this book possible.

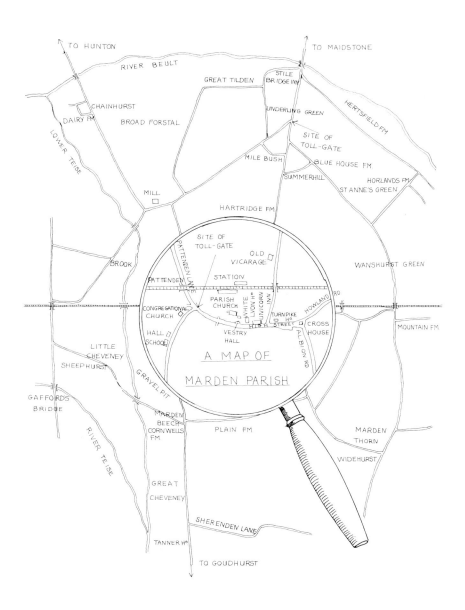

TO HUNTON

TO MAIDSTONE

RIVER BEULT

GREAT TILDEN

STILE
BRIDGE INN

CHAINHURST

UNDERLING GREEN

HERTSFIELD FM

DAIRY FM

BROAD FORSTAL

SITE OF
TOLL-GATE

LOWER TEISE

MILE BUSH

BLUE HOUSE FM

SUMMERHILL

HORLANDS FM
ST ANNE'S GREEN

MILL

HARTRIDGE FM

SITE OF
TOLL-GATE

OLD
VICARAGE

WANSHURST GREEN

BROOK

PATTENDEN LANE

STATION

PATTENDEN

CONGREGATIONAL
CHURCH

PARISH
CHURCH

WHITE H°

LYON H°

UNICORN INN

TURNPIKE
H°

HOWLAND RD

CROSS
HOUSE

MOUNTAIN FM

HIGH STREET

VESTRY
HALL

HALL
SCHOOL

ALBION RD

A MAP OF

LITTLE
CHEVENEY

SHEEPHURST

MARDEN PARISH

GRAVEL PIT

GAFFORDS
BRIDGE

MARDEN
BEECH
CORN WELLS
FM

PLAIN FM

MARDEN
THORN

RIVER TEISE

WIDEHURST

GREAT
CHEVENEY

SHERENDEN LANE

TANNER H°

TO GOUDHURST

A Wealden Village
MARDEN

By

Phyllis Highwood and Peggy Skelton

Illustrations by Robert Highwood

MERESBOROUGH BOOKS
1986

Published by Meresborough Books, 7 Station Road, Rainham, Gillingham, Kent. ME8 7RS.

Meresborough Books is a specialist publisher of books about Kent, founded in 1977 by Hamish & Barbara Mackay Miller. Their list of books in print July 1986 can be found at the back of this book.

ISBN 0948193 107

Printed by Mackays of Chatham Ltd.

CONTENTS

Chapter One

Marden Before 1800

In the history of Kent, the Weald must be reckoned a late developer. While the legions and officials of Rome landed at the ports of Rutupiae (Richborough), Dubris (Dover) or Porta Lemanis (Lympne) and journeyed up Watling Street to London and the other cities of Roman Britain, the great forest of Anderida lay quiet, damp and almost uninhabited. Its small rivers and streams ran tranquilly, little disturbed by man; its trees threaded through with a few tracks and roads.

The Romans did indeed travel through it; one road ran from Rochester to Maidstone, Chart Sutton, Cross at Hand, through Staplehurst, Sissinghurst and down to the Sussex coast, while another linked Benenden, Ashford and Canterbury. Iron was transported along these roads, from iron works in Sussex and also from the Weald, where iron ore and the timber for smelting were available.

Even earlier in the forest there were tracks as men hunted animals and birds. They left some stone axe heads to be picked up in Marden a few thousand years later. A Bronze Age metal worker, too, left his store of bronze on the banks of the river Teise and this was dug up in the late nineteenth century. But there was probably no permanent settlement in those early times. When there was little population pressure, there was no point in living in a cool, wet forest area like Marden if there were lighter, easier soils to the north.

It was after the Romans left, in the so called Dark Ages, that life really began in the Weald. Successive invasions disturbed Kent and eventually a race, which is usually taken to be the Jutes, made a kingdom in Kent. In 'The Jutish Forest' (1976), and more particularly 'The Kingdom of Kent' (1982), K.P. Witney says that the Jutes differed in several ways from the contemporary Angles and Saxons. Four of these distinctions are especially interesting: their freemen had greater liberty; their heirs shared equally in property, that is 'gavelkind', rather than the more usual custom of inheritance by the eldest son; they split their kingdom into provinces or 'lathes' and they lived traditionally in scattered homesteads, not in villages. These customs remained for hundreds of years and helped to shape Kent in a fashion which makes one say of many historical situations, "Well, it was different in Kent".

The kingdom developed in the north and the east, stretching from London, along the north Kent coast roughly to Dover and in the south, along the greensand ridge. It was a small kingdom, but an important one. Ethelbert, a pagan king of Kent whose wife, Ethelburga, was already a christian, welcomed St

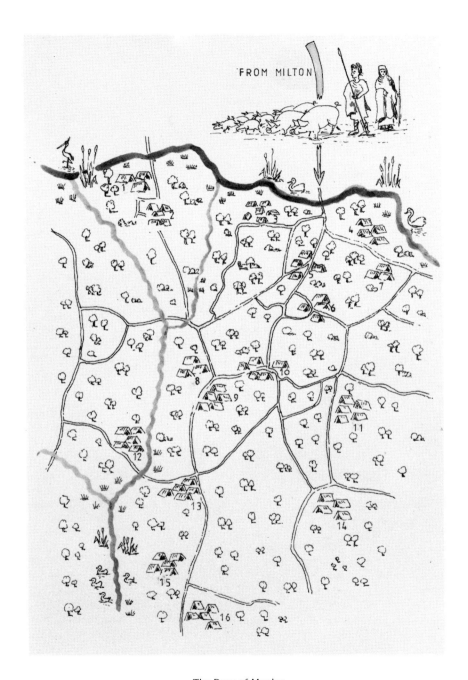

The Dens of Marden

Augustine and his teaching of the gospel into Canterbury in AD 596. By this act Ethelbert influenced the lives of future men of Kent and of Britain.

It was the partitioning of the kingdom of Kent into lathes that brings Marden into this early picture. Some of the lathes belonged to the king himself, others were given to his supporters in return for service. One of the royal possessions was Milton (later Milton Regis) near Sittingbourne which remained crown property until the time of James I who finally sold it off.

As the lathes developed they realised the potential for added wealth which lay in the thick, unknown Weald. They were little interested in Wealden iron, but as herdsmen they discovered that if they took their pigs to feed on the acorns and beech mast for a few weeks each autumn – pannage – their animals fattened better. Each lathe carved out its common land. Milton's was south of the river Beult at Meredenne (Marden). The herdsmen made rough huts, probably in the same place each year, and they may also have made a stockpen. The names of these areas, the 'dens', came about at that time. Some of them remain to this day: Tilden, Bogden, Pattenden and Bisbiche Den (The Beech). Sometimes the herdsmen needed a stop-over den within the common of another lathe in order to reach their own more distant common. Tilden, in the north west of Marden, was just such a den and became the property of the lathe of Aylesford and Maidstone.

Later the lathesmen found that the trees themselves were valuable, for building or for charcoal burning, and the forest began to break up. In this way the lathesmen spent more time in the forest than just a few weeks in autumn. They began to grow crops and permanent communities started.

As settlement increased so the need for churches arose, since all the kings' subjects were expected to get to a church somehow, even if they needed to travel a few miles. There was a church in Marden by about 1085, for it is listed in Domesday Monachorum as a daughter church of Maidstone. It was probably made of wood and could quite likely have been standing when William the Conqueror put to sea in 1066.

Marden is not mentioned by name in the Domesday Book, the great survey of all the property of England, but Milton is recorded. There is mention of a payment by 'the men of the Weald' of fifty shillings and this is generally assumed to refer to Marden, since it appears to have been the only Wealden property Milton possessed.

KEY TO MAP OPPOSITE

1. Reed	9. West Marden
2. Chainhurst (Haydherst)	10. East Marden
3. Tilden	11. Mountain Farm (Monkton)
4. Hertsfield (Hurstfield)	12. Little Cheveney
5. Underlyn (Underden)	13. Beech (Bisbiche Den)
6. St Anne's Green	14. Opp. Thorn (Chilinden)
7. Bogden (Bugindenne)	15. Great Cheveney
8. Pattenden	16. Winchet Hill

Old barn at Great Tilden, before conversion to a house.

High Street looking west. On the left: the Cross House, sixteenth century, where the Courts Leet met until the nineteenth century.

10

Inside the Cross House. The roof timbers.

After the conquest the lathes were divided up into hundreds and the Marden hundred was formed. Hundreds administered the land and held courts. In turn hundreds contained manors, which were often no bigger than a small farm. Under William I Kent developed a manorial system which differed in part from other areas of England. There was no large feudal village, a legacy of the Jutes, but the manor held a 'lord', however minor, who could hold a court, a 'court baron', within his manor to settle his tenants' disputes and to defend his own rights. The land was known as the demesne and part of it was worked by the lord's serfs, but other parts might be let out to even more minor lords who held their land by service to the manorial lord. So long as this service was carried out, the manorial lord could not take back the land. Much of Kent now belonged to the great land-owners: Odo of Bayeux, Earl of Kent (William's half brother); the Abbey of Christ Church, Canterbury; St Augustine's Priory and Battle Abbey. Marden was little changed by this transfer of power, for it still belonged to Milton and there-fore to the crown.

Mediaeval Law and Order

One of Edward Furley's most telling remarks in his 'History of the Weald of Kent' (1874) was: "Marden, though a Royal Hundred and Manor, does not appear to be the most peaceable and honest district in the Weald." He lists crimes of murder, burglary, robbery and larceny, all of which appeared at a

11

single Assize held in Canterbury in 1279. In addition, the bailiff of Marden was charged with cutting down thirty two oaks, the property of the king, to make charcoal. A few years later, in 1309, the men of Tilden and Chainhurst headed, with two hundred and fifty trees, the list of offenders from all over the Weald who cut down timber belonging to the Archbishop of Canterbury. In 1317 Queen Margaret, wife of Edward II (1307-1327), complained that men in Marden and other places took her fish, trees, hares, rabbits, pheasants and partridges. Distant possessions were evidently fair game and worth the occasional prosecution.

By this time Marden hundred was evidently sizeable with a growing population. Edward I (1272-1302) had seized the lands of Leeds Castle and had added the parts which were in Staplehurst and Goudhurst to his Marden estate. He also gave Marden to his mother, Queen Eleanor, who asked for and was given the right to hold a weekly market on Tuesdays and an annual fair, a sign of its reasonable prosperity and of the opportunity for greater trade.

But in 1349 the Black Death arrived in Kent, a plague which swept over the whole country killing perhaps one third or more of the population. We do not know how the Weald was affected. As a scattered area the people may have escaped without too much loss of life. On the other hand the disease was a virulent one and death was likely within a few days for those in contact with infected persons.

The Black Death had far reaching social and economic results. In Kent, the custom of gavelkind had enabled all heirs of a piece of land to inherit a small part. After the Plague many small-holdings could fall to one lucky man (or woman), if the rest of the family had died. In this way many former peasants became independent yeomen with a little more money in their purses. Equally, labourers were now scarce and wages rose to attract those who were available. At the same time the demand for products dropped as the population level plummeted.

In order to help the merchants, whose livelihoods were threatened, the Statute of Labourers was passed, pegging wages to the rate they were before the Black Death. The murmurings of discontent this caused were one of the contributory factors to the other great event of the fourteenth century — the Peasants' Revolt in 1381.

It was not strictly a 'peasants' rising, more the strivings of an artisan group fretting at the ties put upon their trade and liberty. Growing prosperity, however relative, is often the goad which impels men to look for more rights and power. It is interesting to note that when the peasants entered London they killed many Flemings, those immigrants who, with royal assistance, had set up their cloth trade and who might be seen by jealous Kentish eyes (and those of other counties) to have more than their fair share of the limited potential wealth.

There were ten ringleaders who came from the Weald, but none from Marden. Perhaps some of the Marden men walked the few miles to Maidstone where Wat Tyler and John Ball gathered part of their rebellious party, or even followed them to Blackheath where the young king, Richard II (1377-1399), rode out to promise that their lot would be improved. We do know that in September of that same year John Monselow of Marden was one of a group brought to trial at Westminster, accused of plotting on Boughton Heath to burn down Maidstone and force the inhabitants (presumably those who survived the fire) to support the conspirators in making the king keep the pledges he had made at Blackheath. These had never been implemented. And — so they plotted — if the king would not grant the promised charters, they would kill him and his knights. Of the several accused, John Monselow was the only one who was judged Not Guilty. All the rest were sentenced to death and the chief conspirator, Thomas Hardyng of Linton, a mason, had his head spiked on the gate of the palace of Westminster. (W.E. Flaherty. Arch. Cant. Vol. 4.)

It has been said that the memory of risings lingers on in an area and certainly Kent appears to have had the habit of protest. In the next century, the fifteenth, discontent bubbled and overflowed again in the county and in the Weald as it supported the mysterious Jack Cade. This time the grievances were against the inadequate Henry VI. People complained that citizens were indicted as an excuse for the Crown to seize their lands; that the king's household did not pay its bills, that rumour said the king was planning to lay waste the whole of Kent because he thought the men of the county had murdered the Earl of Suffolk. And so it fermented until the march to London began again. W. Durrant Cooper, in his article in Archaeologia Cantiana (1868) says that "In several hundreds the constable duly, and as if legally, summoned the men; and many parishes, particularly Marden, Penshurst (belonging to the Duke of Buckingham), Hawkhurst, Northfleet, Boughton Malherbe, Smarden and Pluckley, furnished as many men as could be found in our own day, fit for arms". Once again, there were no prominent leaders among the men of Marden (there appears to be an art in Marden of joining in any dispute with vigour, but at the same time of keeping the head well down) but John Rolf and John Nash, both yeomen, and Thomas Peppymbury, husbandman, 'and others', all of Marden, were among those pardoned after the affair had petered out. (Cal. Pat. Rolls Henry VI Vol. V.)

The third important rising, which again was almost restricted to Kent, was the Wyatt rebellion of 1554. Queen Mary married Philip of Spain and, although Sir Thomas Wyatt of Allington Castle declared he wished the Queen no ill, he could not stomach a Spanish consort. He tried to co-ordinate risings from several parts of the country, but in the end he and his supporters were left to fight alone. Two of the chief henchmen were Sir Henry Isley and his brother, Thomas, who were both executed at Maidstone along with Sir Thomas Wyatt. Sir Henry owned Reed Court, Marden at that time and the land was then given to Sir John Baker, the Attorney General.

White Lyon House, reputedly the oldest house in Marden.

Turnpike House, formerly a butcher's shop.

The Cloth Trade

Meanwhile, how, apart from growing food, was Marden earning its living? There were signs — the market, the fair, the involvement in outside affairs — that Marden was now an established community. Probably the village owed its relative well-being to an act of Edward III in 1336, when he invited continental cloth workers, especially Flemings, to bring their textile expertise and set up their industry in England. John Kemp settled in Cranbrook and started his trade there. The Weald was a particularly suitable area for cloth, for not only did it have a growing population, but it had abundant timber for fuel and a mass of streams to provide water and water power. Marden eventually had two mills: one in Sheephurst Lane and the other at Pattenden. When they were built is not known, but a map of 1680 refers to the Sheephurst one. Kent could also provide plenty of cloth's raw material — wool.

The king, anxious to nurture the infant industry, passed laws to protect it: no wool was to be exported, nor fuller's earth, an essential product for 'fulling' or cleansing the cloth. No-one was to wear imported cloth. Despite the inevitable smuggling these laws appear to have stimulated a successful industry.

The trade was strictly regulated. Each cloth was sealed (taxed) by an official known as an alnager who inspected every piece of finished cloth — and only sealed cloths could be sold. (In 1353 the tax was four pence a cloth plus a half penny for the alnager.) Each piece of broadcloth measured about thirty to thirty-four yards in length and was rather narrower, fifty inches wide, than cloth of other counties. The weight of the cloth was governed, too, and this varied from sixty-six pounds to eighty pounds over the whole period of the cloth trade in Kent.

The clothier was the mainspring of the industry; he supervised the entire enterprise, from taking the wool to be carded and spun, to delivering it to the weavers and organising the fulling. Fulling or washing had to be done to remove the grease, or lanolin, which the sheep's wool contained. The cloth was put into a tank of water and fuller's earth and either men 'walked' it or it was beaten by hammers driven by water power. Sometimes the cloth was dyed at that stage and at other times the woollen thread was dyed before weaving. After fulling, the cloth was stretched on tenters to dry. Finally the piece was brushed all over with teazles and the shearman trimmed all the loose threads. Kentish cloth was famous all over England and was exported to Europe.

For several hundred years, well into the seventeen hundreds, this industry supported Marden. Its profitability varied according to demand and foreign competition, but, as a petition to Lord Cobham in 1575 pointed out, without the cloth trade many people would have gone hungry.

" . . . there is made within the Weald of Kent yearly by estimation 11,000 or 12,000 cloths. Out of every cloth there groweth to the poor for their relief and living as to spinners, weavers and thickers, fifty shillings; which amounteth to twenty five or twenty six thousand pounds among them yearly.

Wealden type house at Underling Green.

Great Cheveney, started in the sixteenth century and enlarged over the next three centuries. At one time the home of the Maplesden family, clothiers.

. . . the said places in the said county (Kent) where clothing is commonly used is so populous, that the soil thereof is not able by any increase thereof to maintain and find the one half of the inhabitants, except clothing be maintained."

The Weald population was fairly high by then and farmers often had a hand in some part of the process. Twenty to thirty men, women and children might be busy in the making of one cloth.

Many clothiers figure in Marden records, particularly in the seventeenth century when the industry was at its height: James Osborne, Richard Cowtchman, Thomas Burden, Thomas and Richard Willarde, Abraham Whyte, Thomas Cornwell and, of course, the Maplesden family, who became wealthy. Not that

16

Pattenden circa 1920.

prosperity always brought respectability: Thomas Burden was indicted for 'lewd' behaviour, Richard Cowtchman was found guilty of the murder of a Staplehurst clothier, Walter Tourner, in 1601/2. Cowtchman subsequently escaped with the help of his fellow villagers.

In 1640 three clothiers from Marden and Goudhurst invented a new process of dyeing. In the opinion of those who saw a demonstration, clothiers would be "greatly benefited in their trade, repairing generally the reputation which our clothiers, merchants and drapers have lost at home and abroad. It will also save well nigh half the fuel formerly spent." Cloth was at that time going through one of its bad spells, indeed exports had dropped so alarmingly that an enquiry had been set up a few years before to discover why. One of the opinions given in the report was that "deceits in the making and dyeing of English cloth made it unacceptable to the overseas buyers".

Three vats were to be established in Kent to use the new process, though unfortunately there is no trace of whether these came about or, if they did, where they were. An interesting point about this document is its date: 1640 and the comment at the bottom.

"If it took success, as they (clothier witnesses) conceived it might, there was not the like things projected for the good of the Commonwealth in any king's days . . . " (Cal. State Papers Dom.) Evidently there was support for the Parliamentarian regime — or possibly someone wished to secure approval for some reason.

There were linen weavers, too, in Marden, from the beginning of the seventeenth century until well into the eighteenth. Flax was grown in the Weald and

The brewhouse at Great Cheveney built around 1630.

Great Tilden with fine old chimney.

18

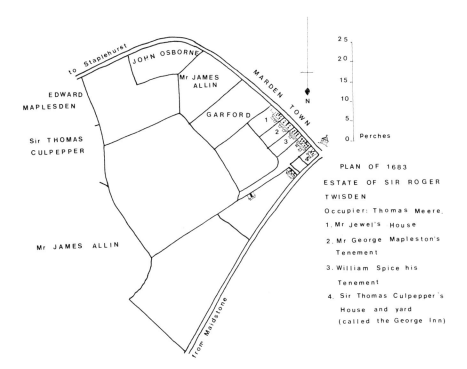

PLAN OF 1683
ESTATE OF SIR ROGER
TWISDEN
Occupier: Thomas Meere.
1. Mr Jewel's House
2. Mr George Mapleston's
   Tenement
3. William Spice his
   Tenement
4. Sir Thomas Culpepper's
   House and yard
   (called the George Inn)

there was a substantial industry in Maidstone (introduced by the immigrant Walloons). There was at least one silk mercer in the second half of the sixteenth century. In 1562 it was noted that the church had silken altar cloths and curtains.

The other great Wealden industry was iron. There is no evidence that Marden took part in this, but there were furnaces nearby at Cranbrook, Goudhurst and Horsmonden. The only mention of the iron trade in Marden is an appeal in 1672 to Maidstone Quarter Sessions for the right to raise a rate to pay for extra labour to repair the roads damaged by ". . . heavy guns and timber". Normally each hundred was responsible for mending the roads and bridges in its immediate area. This was a thorn in most village sides since the men had to give four or six days service a year on road repairs. People who owned land in the village but lived outside often did not bother to turn up or send labour for this unpopular duty. So it may be that the roads were genuinely damaged by heavy transport, or it may have seemed a good opportunity to get out of the hated road service.

To our own eyes, Marden during this period would not appear wealthy, but compared with other villages which had no such industry as the woollen one Marden was certainly reasonably prosperous. The timber framed buildings of today's Marden are signs of its relative well-being. A few houses date from the fifteenth century or earlier, for example White Lyon House. Turnpike House is an example of a 'Wealden' house, with its jettied top storey, as is also a house at

19

Underlyn Farm which has recently been restored. One of the finest houses, which dated back to the end of the fourteenth century, was Great Pattenden. It was occupied by the army during the second world war, neglected afterwards and was eventually demolished. Many houses exist which were erected in the sixteenth and seventeenth centuries, showing how many yeomen and clothiers were able to turn their wealth into solid timber.

Great Cheveney, begun in the sixteenth century, was at one time the home of the Maplesden family, clothiers, a large clan whose name crops up all over the Weald and other parts of Kent. This lovely house was altered and added to in the next three centuries. The brewhouse was built around sixteen hundred. Earlier, in the fourteenth century, Henry del Chyvene held the manor of Chyvene, so presumably there was an even older house.

Another attractive house, Little Cheveney, is also interesting because it belonged to Thomas Twysden who was sent to the Tower by Oliver Cromwell. As a lawyer he defended the rights of the City of London. He served in the Long Parliament and was one of the Commissioners at the trial of those who signed the death warrant of Charles I.

But however splendid these houses still are today, we can appreciate that the smaller dwellings, the cottages, are also the legacy of those who made a successful living from trade or from the land, in the past.

The Church

The church, too, had its share of expansion. There is now no trace of the Saxon, probably wooden, building. The earliest part is the chancel arch, constructed about 1200, shortly after the church had been given (together with Newington) to Lesnes Abbey in north west Kent in 1178, in whose patronage it remained until Cardinal Wolsey suppressed the Abbey in 1524. Wolsey gave the Abbey's possessions to the college he had founded at Oxford, Cardinal College. After Wolsey's disgrace, the property passed briefly to Shere Carthusian monastery in Surrey, but it was Crown property again by 1550, in the reign of Edward VI. It was Queen Elizabeth I, Hasted says, who granted Marden church (amongst others) to the see of Canterbury in the early days of her reign. However, the vicars appear to have enjoyed royal patronage up to the appointment of John Wood MA in 1614, in the reign of James I. (The Register of Archbishop Abbot.)

By the fifteenth century the church began to look more as it does today: the chapel of St John the Baptist had been built on the north side and on the south there was a porch with a parvise (small room) above, added to the south aisle.

It is surprising that in the midst of all this construction both in the church and in the village itself, that the church became a place of neglect. In 1556/7 the chancel burned down and for decades afterwards there was no chancel roof. Discolouration from the fire can still be seen in the south wall of the Lady Chapel today.

Several years later, in 1573, Archbishop Parker reported after a Visitation to Marden:

" . . . there Channcell was burned in the 2/3 yere of Queen Mary and yerely hath been presented, but reformacon (repair) they have none, wych yf they cannot have they must be dryven to sewe to the Councell, for the parishioners are so annoyed for lack of Rowme (room) that many therefore comme not to Church as they shulde."

The Archbishop went on " . . . they have sermons, but not at the appointment of there Vicar, but by the procurement of the parishioners, there Vicar is absent and hath lett his benefice to a Curate."

Thirty years before the Archbishop's visit, Archbishop Cranmer had written in a volume dealing with 'The Heretics of Kent' that "These towns are specially to be remembered that in them be placed learned men with sufficient stipends: Sittingbourne, Dover, Folkestone, Ashford, Tenterden, Cranbrook, Faversham, Herne, Whitstable, Marden, Maidstone, Wye and Wingham."

Evidently no-one had taken Cranmer's advice and it is quite likely that the sermons enjoyed by the parishioners were as 'heretical' as Cranmer had feared, for the paying of non-conformist preachers to give sermons was just beginning to become popular; the Weald had long had a reputation for such tendencies.

Marden lost its church plate in Edward VI's reign, when many churches were robbed of their valuables to provide money for the royal purse. The plate included: two chalices, two patens and a pax of silver and parcel gilt, 32 ounces; one pair of censers, silver parcel gilt, 19 ounces, one pax, silver and parcel gilt, 12 ounces. It totalled 63 ounces. Queen Mary did restore some plate to churches when she came to the throne, but Marden's was 'defaced' when it was checked into the Jewel House — probably melted down — and was certainly missing for the Visitation in 1573. Or did the astute villagers put out for Archbishop Parker's benefit only " . . . a glass for Lacke of a Commonion Cuppe . . . " just in case Queen Elizabeth felt the need of a donation?

Eleven years after this Visitation, Salomon Boxer arrived as vicar. Although it was complained that he cheated a parishioner of some money and allowed his cows to wander round the church yard, at least he was on the job for the next thirty years until he died in 1614.

Like many other parishes in Kent, Marden church remained in the care of an Anglican vicar for some time during the Commonwealth. John Wood MA followed Salomon Boxer, in 1614, and stayed until his death in 1643. That was the year that all adults were required to sign the Covenant in support of the Parliamentarian party and to swear that they would not help any army raised by the king (Charles I). The lists of those who signed were to be supervised by the ministers and kept in church. There is no trace of one in Marden. After John Wood's death, the list of ministers is rather confused and there are gaps in the registers. In 1644 another (or the same?) Mr Wood 'Vicar of Marden' was buried. Gabriel Price's name appears also in 1644, then Matthias Sympson in 1648-1652 and Christopher Blackwood 1651/2. There is a curious entry in the Baptism register in 1644: "Jane and Eliz. of Jeffery and Eliz. Jarvaise, at Linton Church, yet having three ministers at Marden".

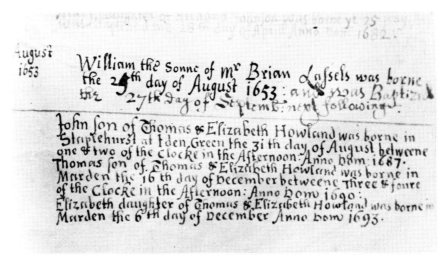

An entry of 1653 in the Church Register. The lower entry is interesting: does the Howland Road derive its name from this family?

Before the Restoration of Charles II in 1660, George Amhurst, Anglican, was inducted in 1657. He remained minister for fifty years, until 1707. In the Crompton Census of Religion of 1672, Marden is listed as having 669 conformists (C of E), 1 Papist (unknown) and 30 non-conformists. If these figures are true (and this must always be in doubt), they are a little surprising, for the figures of the neighbouring parishes are rather different:

Goudhurst 900 conformists   100 non-conformists
Staplehurst 295 conformists   160 non-conformists

A possible explanation might be (if this was a true picture of Marden's religious life) that after several ministers in the short period between 1643 and 1657, the advent of George Amhurst, Anglican, (however 'low' he may have been) had, by 1672, given the village fifteen years of stability and had assured the church of its congregation.

The Care of the Poor and the Workings of the Vestry

Marden entered the eighteenth century with its clothiers still working their trade, but during the hundred years that followed, the industry gradually died out in the village and in Kent in general, moving westwards and eventually northwards. There was still money in the parish, however, for records show a fair number of men who were styled 'gentleman' in the church registers. The substantial houses we have noted needed substantial men to maintain them.

On the other hand, there were as ever the poor, the infirm and the elderly. In the age of the monasteries these people were fed and clothed by the monks

22

– little or much, according to the conscience of the monastery. After the Dissolution of the monasteries, beggars, drop-outs and returning soldiers (there was always a war somewhere) created such havoc that in Queen Elizabeth I's reign each parish became and remained responsible in law for any welfare help necessary for all the people born within its boundaries, wherever they might move.

A group of parishioners of standing were made Overseers of the Poor and they looked after those in need, with money raised by a rate on all who owned a house or land. Marden's Overseers built a Poorhouse or Workhouse (both names are used) where Allen's now stands, for those without any means of supporting themselves at home. Others were helped with extra money, clothes or other requirements; that kind of help was more general before 1834 and the New Poor Law Amendment Act. Sometimes a poor child was apprenticed to a master either in the village, or better still (from the Overseers' point of view) outside since apprenticeships often specified transferring settlement responsibility to the apprentice's new parish, which meant that there was no risk of that child becoming a charge on the parish in later life. After 1691 this transferring became automatic and Marden apprenticed several children out of the village in the eighteenth century. The illustrated indenture is interesting because of the name of the child: George Maplesden, a reminder that however wealthy a family might be, there is usually a penniless offshoot somewhere.

The Overseers were appointed by the Vestry, a body of people who did the work of a modern parish council, church council and welfare committee. It met in the church or, more comfortably, at White Lyon House just up the road. Most of the affairs of the village and the church were arranged by the Vestry, of whom the vicar and churchwardens were members.

In 1735 they had to deal with the gifts of Mrs Mary Allen and her son, John, who both left money in their wills to the 'Poor of Marden'. The Vestry decided, with the addition of money raised on loan, to buy the complete piece of land at Appledore, formerly owned by the Allens " . . . for the better settling and securing The Gift . . . " Although the land was sold off in this century there is still a small amount of money, linked with the money left by Edward Maplesden on land at Horsmonden, which today forms the Allen and Maplesden Charity.

In the same year the Vestry decided to make a suit in Common Law against Richard Pollard, at its own expense, on behalf of the widow Mary Adams, for " . . . fraudulent taking her goods and other ill usage". Again in that year they found that one of the rooms in the Poorhouse could be spared and they resolved to engage a school master " . . . to teach and instruct Youth in writing, reading and Arithmetic during the Pleasure of the Parish".

For several years in the middle of the century the poor state of the church bells and their frames worried the Vestry. In 1738 they thought that since four of the five bells were damaged, it would be a good idea to have them recast, with the addition of more metal, into five, so that with the remaining sound one they would have a peal of six. For the next seven years they passed unanimous

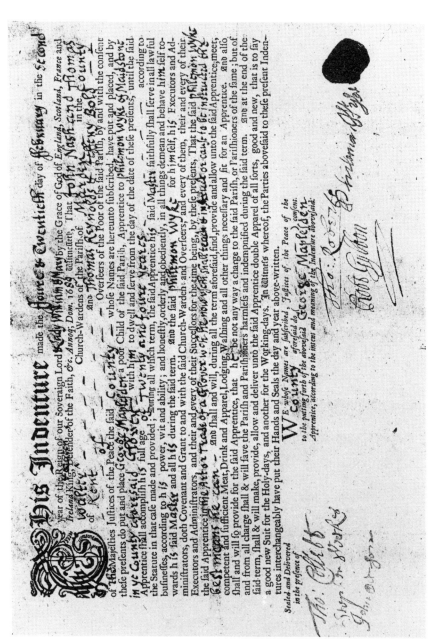

The Indenture certificate of George Maplesden, a poor child, who was apprenticed to Philemon Wyke, Glover, of Maidstone, until he should reach the age of twenty four. 1689. KAO P 244 14. (From 'The Poor', Kentish Sources, by kind permission of the Kent Archives Off.)

resolutions to do just that, but evidently found the expense daunting. Eventually two bells were made in 1745 and one each in 1758, 1775 and 1777. The number one bell of the new peal bore the following inscription:

"Thomas Lester made me 1745.
At proper times my voice I will raise
And sound to my subscriber's praise."

The bells, including the old 1693 one, lasted until 1909, when they were again recast.

One other duty of the Vestry was to supervise the repairing of the roads when necessary and to organise the rate which paid for the materials and labour. It also negotiated with the Turnpike Trust commissioners when the Turnpike roads were built; these were first mentioned in 1764 and were built before 1780. One road ran from Maidstone via Stile Bridge through Staplehurst to Cranbrook and the other one went from Stile Bridge through the village up to Goudhurst.

The Vestry was not always a united body; it had its controversial moments. In 1774 the Rev. John Andrews, vicar, tried to have his choice of People's churchwarden, William Watts, re-elected at the Easter Vestry. However, most of the Vestry voted against Watts. At a subsequent Visitation the Archdeacon had to declare the election null. At a poll carried out a few weeks later the public Vestry meeting was enlarged from an average dozen people to an astonishing sixty-two. The vicar had to admit defeat and the parishioners' choice, John Burr, was elected.

So the village had developed through eight or nine hundred years, from an uncultivated piece of forest where pigs rooted for a few weeks in the year to a settled community, with a church, at least two schools (Sir Charles Booth had left money for the founding of a school in 1796, in addition to the one in the Poorhouse; there may have been others), substantial houses and farms.

It had endured the comparative poverty of most non-industrialised societies; it had suffered the Black Death and the three hundred years or so of intermittent outbreaks of plague which had followed. It had benefited from the cloth trade and had lived through its frequent slumps.

The village had brushed with authority, existed through serfdom and oppression and had emerged at the end of the eighteenth century with about sixteen hundred inhabitants, most of whom could earn some sort of living if they were able bodied. It was by no means an isolated place. People moved freely round the villages and into Maidstone; they went visiting, courted their wives, sold their stock and produce, had a day at a fair or looked for work elsewhere. Even crime spread round the parishes; the West Kent Assize records are full of misdeeds committed by Marden men in other villages and of men from outside Marden who stood surety for Marden malefactors. It is evident, too, that rebellion and religious ideas suffused the Wealden area as a plant absorbs water.

Chapter Two

The Period Before Mechanisation

Marden in 1800

In 1800, at the beginning of the new century, Marden was an agricultural community. There was a turnpike road to Goudhurst, as noted above, and this was presumably a reasonable road. Edward Hasted writing in his 'History and Topographical Survey of the County of Kent (1797-1801) took a poor view of the other roads in the parish, which in winter were muddy and at times impassable.

William Marshall, too, describing a journey he took in the Weald to produce his 'Rural Economy of the Southern Counties' (1797), found Wealden roads in general " . . . such that no man who has not stept out of his cradle can travel without disgust: if he can travel without danger". Indeed, although the Weald and Maidstone were important suppliers of food and hops to London, the roads must have placed certain limitations on trade.

Marshall thought the 'townships' of the Weald were very large. (Maidstone numbered about eight thousand people at this time). There were about three hundred houses in Marden, many of which, Hasted wrote, were "but meanly built", but he conceded that the farm houses were "antient, well-timbered". The village was largely self-supporting: local craftsmen could have supplied the houses, barns, clothes, shoes, tools and harness. Queen Eleanor's market had lapsed by this time but there was still an annual fair in October for toys and pedlary. There were fairs at Maidstone and Cranbrook to attract the village. Maidstone was only about eight miles away — within walking distance in fair weather, or even quicker by horse if one's pockets were full.

In 1800 thirty-five children were brought to church to be baptised; eight children died, along with twenty-four adults, the third highest death rate in the ten years since 1790. The vicar who buried them was still the Rev. John Andrews LL B, who had had such trouble with his churchwardens in 1774. He must have been sympathetic towards free church practices because he gave a house to be used by visiting non-conformist ministers to preach the gospel. With the gift of another house shortly afterwards, this became the beginning of the Congregational church and Manse.

Sir Charles Booth's school had only been in existence for four years and compulsory education did not become law until 1870, so most people at that time could not read or write with ease. Of nine couples who married in church, only seven people could sign their names in the register; the others had to make a mark.

This was Marden at the beginning of the century that was to see so much change. George III, his American colonies lost, sat on the English throne, Napoleon still strove to dominate Europe; Marden men served in the West Kent Regiment of Militia; Parliament was little known, for only a few Marden men had the vote. Pitt had tried to initiate electoral reform, but most of those in power were nervous of events in France: it was only six years after 'The Terror'.

Another kind of revolution, though, was shaking parts of Britain. Steam engines, stationary at the moment, were starting to convert the country from an agricultural community into an industrial nation. Factories in the north were turning out wool and cotton on machines powered by steam.

But all that was far from Marden. Its daily life and future were, for quite a while, to be bound up with the land.

Farming in the First Half of the Nineteenth Century

Although farming was the mainstay of the Weald in the first half of the nineteenth century, at least one observer was doubtful about its suitability and success. William Marshall, as he endured the poor roads at the end of the eighteenth century to report on the soil and farming practices of the Weald, was not entirely pleased with what he saw, presumably compared with his experiences on his journeys elsewhere. He found there were " ... many foul lands ... the proportion of arable lands appeared to be much too great ... the hedgerows were far too high, wide and impervious to the winds for a low, dirty arable country". The earth was " ... a pale adhesive clay ... " but around Marden " ... a clay of a higher colour and richer quality prevails while on the rising ground on which the village of Staplehurst is judiciously placed, is much of it of a warmer, more genial nature, a good clayey loam".

The soil needed lightening and manuring; generally the men of the Weald took lime from the North Downs. Marshall said that the practice was so widespread that, when viewed from a height in autumn, the whole valley looked mottled. The other dressing used was 'marl', which is thought to be an impure kind of fullers' earth. Earlier it had been seen by the clothiers as a cheaper substitute for the high quality but expensive fullers' earth supplied from Boxley, near Maidstone.

There were very few orchards in the Weald in Marshall's day (or for quite a time afterwards) " ... the most were in the township of Marden and these were of apples, a species of fruit which is ill-adapted to the Weald lands. The pear would probably flourish on many of them." He does not say why he thought apples unsuitable; he might have thought the soil too wet or that such a low lying area was vulnerable to frost – which is true. He would no doubt be surprised by the amount of apples marketed from Marden today.

Marshall approved of the cattle he saw in the parish " ... and in Marden cows of the fairest mould, wearing every appearance in form color and horn of being

27

Parish of *Marden* — *Kent* — in the Diocese of *Canterbury*

	Number of Acres.	GENERAL REMARKS.
Wheat . . .	600	*In this parish crops of everykind*
Barley . . .	60	*have been exceedingly abundant:* *particularly hops. There are near*
Oats . . .	500	*six hundred Acres of hop-ground*
Potatoes . . .	30	*in this parish. Notwithstanding,* *the poor-rates, if something is*
Peas . . .	150	*not done, will in a few years* *prove our ruin: they check the*
Beans . . .	100	*spirit of industry among the poor,*
Turnips or Rape .	30	*and we shall soon have no La-* *bourers to till our Lands. I*
Rye	None.	*aver this on my own know-* *ledge, as a Magistrate of the* *County. J. Andrews, etc.r*

Details of crop acreages in Marden in 1801. This report sent by the Rev. John Andrews in response to the Archbishop's request for such information throughout the diocese. HO 64/4. PRO Kew.

of the purest blood, of the middle-horned race of cattle". They were Sussex cattle, he said, and oxen were used as draft beasts. There had been Kentish cattle in earlier times, still red. Daniel Defoe in 'A Tour Through the Whole Island of Great Britain' (1724) had described those he saw in Maidstone market as coming from the Wild (Weald) of Kent, " . . . which begins but about six miles off and particularly from that part which lies this way; they bring the large Kentish bullocks, famed for being generally all red and with their horns crooked inward, the two points directly against each other. They are counted the largest breed in England".

In Marshall's opinion Marden and Staplehurst grew the largest acreages of hops and Marden continued to be one of the major hop producers during most of the nineteenth century. But evidently at the end of the eighteenth century there had been a marked increase generally in the planting of hops. The vicar of East Malling wrote in 1801 (in a report to the Archbishop of Canterbury) "The Plantation of Hops is of late so great in this county especially that the quantity of grain is of course greatly diminished, insomuch that instead of the usual number of acres in each Parish that used to have about 140 or 150 acres is now advanced to 600".

Marden in 1801 (according to the Rev. John Andrews' own return to the Archbishop) had nearly six hundred acres of hops. There are no earlier figures so we cannot tell whether Marden had enlarged its hop growth or not. The other 1801 figures were:

Wheat	600 acres	Peas	150 acres
Barley	60 acres	Beans	100 acres
Oats	500 acres	Turnips or rape	50 acres
Potatoes	30 acres	Rye	none

These figures are probably rounded up but they give an idea of the proportion of the various crops. The figure for wheat, 600 acres, appears quite high, but an acre would produce less than a ton even in a good year and considerably less in a poor one. An acre of wheat today would yield an average three tons. Most people in 1801 would eat a large amount of bread, as the mainstay of their diet, so consumption would be high in each family. It is doubtful whether the parish could supply all its wheat needs as the population grew during the century.

On the other hand, the large acreage of a cash crop – hops – would probably ensure that wheat could be bought in if necessary. Hop growing was an uncertain occupation – the yields fluctuated in a spectacular manner from year to year as the plants fell victim to red spider, aphis and mould, for which there were no cures. A hundredweight of hops might be worth £10 one year and £3 the next. But the fact that Marden maintained a large growth throughout the century must have made what Cobbett in his 'Rural Rides' (1830) called "a gambling concern" worthwhile.

In 1824 hop acreages were:

Marden	401 acres	Headcorn	133 acres
Staplehurst	190½ acres	Frittenden	131 acres
Goudhurst	241 acres	Benenden	358½ acres
Cranbrook	491 acres	Hawkhurst	355 acres
Horsmonden	241 acres	Maidstone	418 acres
		Yalding	770 acres

Later in the century the acreage rose, reaching its highest point in the 1880s.

The hops were grown on poles. In early spring three or four poles, from ten to sixteen feet long, were put into each 'hill' (where the hop crown grew: 1,000 hills to an acre). Often farms coppiced their own wood to supply the huge quantity of poles needed. They were made of chestnut (reckoned the most durable) or of ash or beech. Otherwise the farmers bought them about every five to twelve years. When they were no longer fit for the hop-garden they were cut up and used to make some of the charcoal the dryer needed. In the winter the men stacked the poles into wigwams of three to four hundred each.

As the hops grew they had to be trained. The trainers visited each hill three times during the early growing season. They encouraged the hops to climb clockwise round the poles, tying them on with fresh rushes.

The soil was weeded and aerated and for this the men used a nidget or shim, a horse drawn cultivator with long iron tines. In some places this was still done by hand.

Hop-picking was a time of general effort. Labourers' wives, farmers' wives and children all helped to get the hops in before they spoiled. Drying had originally been carried out in the lofts of small barns, even house attics, but as acreages grew separate oast houses were built, with a kiln and a cooling floor. The hops were dried over charcoal fires, the warm air rising up through the layer of green hops and out through the top of the kiln.

It was recognised in Marshall's day that the most valuable hops were those with the most resin, or 'condition' as it was then known. Male hops were regarded as weeds and were grubbed, though Marshall, rightly, tentatively suggested that all the really good samples of hops he had seen contained seeds. Male hops were later appreciated as a crop enhancer and were planted deliberately.

Each pocket of hops was taxed by the Customs and Excise for well over half of the nineteenth century – a cause of much grumbling among growers. This and the uncertainty of cropping may have been two of the reasons why fruit production finally outstripped that of hops in the twentieth century. Nonetheless, the hop remained, in the first half of the nineteenth century, an important and on the whole lucrative part of the farming scene.

The Poor 1800-1850

In 1801 the Rev. John Andrews had written, " . . . the Poor Rate, if something is not done, will in a few years prove our ruin; they check the spirit of industry among the Poor and we shall soon have no labourers to till our lands".

As a vicar in a good living, his remark sounds singularly unchristian and unrealistic of the benefits of being on Poor Relief. But his comment probably reflected some feelings of his time that help to the needy should not be indulgent. In fact the amount of time and energy devoted to looking after the poor and infirm was considerable. There was probably not much risk that recipients of relief would stop looking for jobs, but the amount of money involved and the extent of the care given to those in need is surprising to our Welfare State orientated minds.

Relief was of two kinds, as noted above: those who had no money or means of supporting themselves would be taken in to the Poorhouse, but relief outside the Poorhouse was common, not only for those who had no work, but also for families, especially large ones, where the man's wages were not enough to feed and clothe his wife and children adequately. Money, clothing, medicines and help in nursing were all given under the Overseers' supervision.

A family of a working man, his wife and three children was expected to be able to provide for itself, but above that number of children in the family, the parish paid (up to 1814) two shillings for every child, per week. If a child earned between three shillings and sixpence and six shillings (18p and 30p), a shilling would be deducted (5p). If the child received more than six shillings, no relief would be given for him. A journeyman tradesman had to have five children to qualify for relief.

Those who thought they should have relief and did not receive it could and did apply to the local magistrates. There are several such records for Marden. This may be why the following entry appears in the Overseers' accounts books: "It being the wish of this Meeting to give the Magistrates as little trouble as possible in hearing complaints from the Poor, it is requested that John Noakes (later noted as Parish Clerk) do state to any of the Paupers who are dissatisfied with the Relief given them, that one of the Overseers will meet them at the next or any subsequent Sitting and explain such Relief". (May 1814)

The Relief was closely supervised: the Overseers kept careful and detailed accounts of all they spent. It seems unlikely that under the system anyone would become destitute, although they might live uncomfortably. There was little question of retirement, for instance. On 1st July 1814, the Overseers decreed that "Old men of seventy who are in the Poorhouse and able to work shall be entitled to Half their Earnings and to be at Liberty to choose their own Masters". On the other hand, those old men who lived under the much harsher regimes of the later nineteenth century workhouses would probably have thought that arrangement a benevolent one. There were several old men in the parish at any time; there were large numbers of child deaths during the nineteenth century, but the registers show a great spread of age with many people reaching their seventies and even eighties and nineties.

If a poor person applied for relief, he was often found work by the Overseers, either on the roads or on local farms. When William Ashdown asked for relief because he had been out of work for several days in the month, the answer was that the Overseers would not " . . . grant any Relief with the like excuse now nor in future; but that any Pauper being out of work should apply to John L. Noakes, who is desired at all times to find work for such as are in want".

They also noted, "It is considered that any Pauper who is known to earn sufficient by his Labour to Clothe his Family, but spends his Money at the Publick House, shall not be allowed any Clothes from the Parish". Charity certainly had its limits.

A parish doctor was appointed who looked after the poor — but again under supervision. In August 1814 Ambrose Daws asked that the doctor attend his wife. The Overseers agreed, but declared that in future no pauper could be visited by the doctor without the prior approval of a Vestry meeting.

The old law of 'Settlement' still applied, even in the nineteenth century. In 1812 a Marden man had been living in Ash for twenty-six years, in a property valued at £9 a year. When for some reason he became a charge on the Poor Rate

A bill to the Parish of Marden from Thomas Sharp:

To Sevendays & Nights to Nursen Young Barns with the small Pox	15s. 0d	
Do for Layen forth	1s. 0d	
Do for a Man one Night to Set up and Help Keep Him in Bead by force	1s. 0d	17s. 0d
More for Licker when put in Cofin & Fecht a way		1s. 0d
		18s. 0d

P 244 18/5

1784

of Ash (through sickness, age or losing a job), the Overseers there applied for a Removal order to send the man, John Wilkins, his wife and child back to Marden, his former place of settlement. The magistrates refused to grant the order because they said the house he lived in was worth £10 a year, which by law cancelled the responsibility of his birth place and entitled him to settlement — and relief — from Ash. Nevertheless, one of the Ash Overseers, a Mr Cox, uprooted the family and abandoned them in Marden, to be taken in by the Marden Overseers. Understandably reluctant to support a family who appeared to have the right to care by another parish, the Overseers commissioned their own survey of Wilkins' house, which confirmed it was over the legal settlement rate. They also sent for advice to the Cranbrook solicitor, Mr Willis. He took counsel's opinion which was that Cox's action was " . . . an impudent attempt to impose a charge, which in point of law could not be imposed". His behaviour, however, was not thought to be indictable for there was no conspiracy, nor was it " . . . a case of any inhumanity in the treatment of the Paupers . . . ".

In the legal sense there was no inhumanity, but the suffering of the family must have been acute. Mr Willis' advice to the Marden Overseers was, "Make the

32

best terms with Cox you can". Unfortunately we do not know what those terms were.

One of the duties which the Rev. John Andrews had to undertake, together with the Overseers, at the turn of the century was to look after the families of the men serving in the West Kent Regiment of Militia. The men were chosen by lot and had to serve five years in the Militia, either in action against an enemy or, in peace time, in quelling local disturbances. If the balloted man did not want to do this, he could produce a suitable substitute who was willing to serve instead. Exchanges went on over several parishes: Marden men took the place of reluctant soldiers from Staplehurst, Hadlow, Yalding, Kingsdown and even as far off as Kenardington. Equally, other parishes provided substitutes for Marden men. The County Treasurer paid relief for the families of the balloted men, and this was also dealt with by the Overseers. For an unemployed man or a poor one, service in the Militia might sometimes appear to be a way of helping the family finances. In 1798 Richard Hunt was selected to serve. At the time he was designated 'pauper', so the lump sum he received on enlistment and the fact that his wife, Lucy, and his two children would have relief from the parish, might well have proved attractive. The Overseers were ordered to pay the family four shillings and sixpence (23p) " . . . being the usual price for 3 days labour in husbandry . . . " At the bottom of the Magistrate's certificate, John Andrews had added, "Lucy Hunt has had third child — therefore require you to pay 1/6 more (8p)".

After war, all countries, both victor and vanquished, suffer as economies take time to adjust to the lower demands for food, clothing and weapons of a peaceful country. Indeed, by 1814, a year before Waterloo, the Marden churchwardens and Overseers were concerned about poor relief, both who should have it and how much it should be. Several families were invited to list their provision needs for a week. Richard Hunt, now with seven children (there had been ten, but three had died), set out his requirements:

8 gall. of flour		12s. (60p)
2ozs tea		1s. 1d. (5p)
4lbs cheese	@ 9d.	3s. (15p)
1¼lbs butter	@ 15d	1s. 6¾d. (8p)
1¼lbs sugar	@ 14d.	1s. 5½d. (8p)
½lb soap	@ 13d.	6½d. (3p)
½lb salt		2½d. (1p)
3lbs meat		2s. 3d. (11p)
Yeast		6d. (3p)
	Total	£1. 3s. 2d. (£1. 16p)

Overleaf:
An order from Lord George Murray JP to the Overseers of Marden to pay maintenance to Lucy Hunt, wife of a balloted man. The Rev. John Andrews' note requests extra money for her because of the birth of her third child. 1798. KAO P 244 17

Hunt

Lucy Hunt.

To the Overseers of the Poor
of the Parish of Marden in the
said County

Whereas Complaint upon oath
hath been made unto me Lord
George Murray one of His Majs
Justices of the Peace for the said
County; by Lucy Hunt now dwelling
in your Parish wife of Richard
Hunt a private militia man
serving in the militia of the
said County as a balloted man
which militia are in actual
service and have been ordered
to march - that she is not
able to support herself and
their Children Sarah aged four
years and Mary aged two years
I do therefore hereby order you
to pay to the said Lucy Hunt
from Monday the 12th day of the
present month the weekly sum
of four Shillings and Sixpence
for the support of her and her
said children being the usual
price of three days labour in
husbandry within the said Coun

or forthwith to shew me cause to the contrary; which weekly sum is to be reimbursed to you by the Treasurer of the said County; who is hereby required to reimburse the same accordingly.

Given under my hand and seal the 22nd day of March in the year of our Lord 1798

George Murray

Whereas the within-named Lucy Hunt has been lately delivered of a third child, named Betty. These are therefore to require you to pay to sd Lucy Hunt One shilling and Sixpence pr week more than the above allowance of four & sixpence; from the day of the date hereof. Given under my hand this 14th day of July 1798

J Andrews.

35

Against this he set the amount he received:

Himself for labour	(per week)	18s. 0d. (a high rate) (90p)
-do- for wife		— —
-do- for Boy		4s. 0d. (20p)
-do- for relief for 28 weeks		£7. 15s. 6d. (£7.78p)
-do- for Clothes for 28 weeks		£2. 16s. 10d. (£2.84p)
-do- for Shoes for 28 weeks		£1. 6s. 6d. (£1.33p)

In 1814 Richard Hunt, even with seven children, probably managed fairly well, for the Overseers had noted in that year that the day rate for labour would continue at 2s. 6d. (13p). But when wages sank after the Napoleonic wars were over, to below two shillings, he would have had a struggle. In addition, in August 1814, the Overseers decided to lower the rate of relief and John Noakes was sent off to Cranbrook to the next Sitting of the Magistrates to see what other parishes were paying their paupers.

The Overseers and the committee which helped them learned that other parishes had only been paying one shilling and sixpence (8p) when Marden was paying two shillings. They resolved to continue for the time being to relieve at the full rate all those who generally paid their rents regularly; but to cut, often by half, the relief to those whose rents were already paid by the Parish, ie the very poor. They also stopped the clothing allowance except for a real emergency.

This solution to falling funds must have caused suffering, but it might be seen in the spirit of the self-help tradition of the age and of the lessening prosperity of those who had to find the money to relieve the poor. For not only did wages sink after the war, but prices did too. In 1813 wheat had sold at 109s. 6d. per quarter (£5.48p per 504lbs); on 3rd January 1815 it fell to 65s. 0½d. (£3.25p) (Maidstone Journal). Certainly the 1813 price was an inflated one, but it had allowed wages to rise (the 1814 rate was 2s. 6d. per day as noted) and the farmers to pay their rents more readily – and the Poor Rate.

In March 1815 Parliament passed a Corn Law to protect the price of corn. Foreign grain could only be imported when the home product reached eighty shillings a quarter. This was very unpopular with all sections of society except landowners and farmers. Angry Londoners broke some windows in the Palace of Westminster until quelled by the Horse Guards, while in Maidstone one of the members of Parliament, Earl Darnley of Cobham, had to retreat from an open meeting in the town to the Bell Inn because of " . . . the dreadful tumult of the populace". In the safety of the inn he declared he was proud to have defended the interests of the farmers by voting for the Corn Law " . . . notwithstanding all the clamour and ill-treatment of a misguided mob, whose ideas of the question will prove their ruin". (Maidstone Journal). It was the beginning of a time of hardship for all but a few privileged people.

Meanwhile, the Overseers of Marden had organised the village into four quarters and had welcomed a committee who would be in charge of the four areas, in their job of looking after the poor. These divisions were:

Beech Quarter: James Barton and Edward Love
Pattenden Quarter: James Gladish and William Hayes
Town Quarter: John Osborne and Alexander Selby
Wanshurst Quarter: William Shoebridge and William Austen Jnr.

The committee members were to attend every meeting or to forfeit two shillings and sixpence (13p) for each absence. If they averaged four meetings out of every five they would be entitled to a dinner on Easter Monday. They would each be allowed five shillings out of the Parish rates for the dinner, but if they wanted wine, it would be paid for out of the forfeit money. William Hayes ensured at least some wine by missing the second meeting of the year.

One of the difficulties this body faced was that of gathering in the considerable amount of money it disbursed yearly. Every house and every piece of land in the village was rated according to its rental value. Some people like James Day, a little later, whose rents added up to £124.5s. (£124.25p) might pay £12. 8s. 6d. (£12.43p) on a two shilling rate, while Charlotte Walter, whose cottage had a rental value of £1 would pay 2s. (10p). But setting a Poor Rate was one thing and getting the money in was quite another. There were always ratepayers in arrears and this led to the following note in May 1814:

"In consideration of the difficulty experienced by the late Overseers in collecting the Poor Rate, it is thought just and proper that the following Rules should be observed and that the present Overseers be recommended so to do – That Non-Residents and Persons who hold Tyburn Tickets, or from any other cause are exempt from serving Parish Offices, shall be the first called on to Pay their Poor Rate and that the Overseers and the Committee for the time being should be the last."

Holders of Tyburn Tickets were those who had prosecuted someone who was later convicted of the felony; they were then excused all Parish offices as a kind of reward – but this evidently made little impression on the Overseers. As another practical footnote the Overseers added: "It is understood and allowed that the Overseers for the time being shall have such Persons in the Poorhouse/and are able to go/for Hoping (hop-picking), by paying them as others are paid".

With six hundred acres of hops to pick in the parish, the advantage of first offer of extra labour was a perk worth having; one feels that the hard-pressed Overseers deserved it.

The following year, 1815, for instance, brought not only Waterloo, but a large batch of children into the village, which probably meant an even greater demand on the Poor Rate. Ninety-three babies were baptised within the year, many more than usual.

1810	41 babies baptised		1814	60	babies	baptised
1811	56 "	"	1815	93	"	"
1812	62 "	"	1816	54	"	"
1813	63 "	"	1817	64	"	"

It might have been caused by the husbands returning from army service, but a note from the Overseers suggests this was not so, for in January they wrote: "It is agreed that all Girls who are pregnant and who apply for Relief shall come into the Poor House unless they can maintain themselves".

The Parish continued to be responsible for the Poor and to help them in any way they found suitable until the passing of the New Poor Law Amendment Act of 1834, when parishes were grouped together in Unions and a joint Poorhouse, often with harsh conditions, was used by the villages. The intention of the Act was evidently to lower the Poor Rates by cutting outdoor relief, encouraging farmers to raise wages, and making the Union Poorhouse a place where only those without any hope of support would apply to enter.

Marden belonged to the Maidstone Union (district 2, together with Staplehurst, Linton, Bearsted, Otham and Boughton Monchelsea), whose Poorhouse was at Coxheath. But outdoor relief within the parish continued, almost as though, financially pressed as it certainly was, the village was reluctant to give up responsibility for its own. In 1836 the old Poorhouse was put up for sale, since it was then unoccupied, but two years later it was decided to repair it; it was later used as a tenement for the poor who were not destitute enough to go 'up the Union'.

That there was continued concern for the low wage earners is shown by this notice which, it was noted in the Vestry book, was fixed to the main church door — where it could not fail to catch the vicar's eye, in 1839. The vicar was the Rev. Philip Le Geyt.

"Notice is hereby given of a meeting to be held on 9th of January for the purpose of taking into consideration the propriety of raising a Fund or a Voluntary Rate for the Relief of Large Families that cannot under the existing Law, be Relieved from the Poor Rate. Signed Stephen Walter."

On the day of the proposed meeting, Stephen Walter wrote in the Vestry Book: "Mr Le Geyt having been previously applied to upon this subject and his answer not received and there also being only a small number of parishioners present it was considered advisable to adjourn the Meeting . . . "

Philip Le Geyt does not appear to have been particularly sympathetic towards the poor, either on that occasion or earlier, during the Agricultural Riots of 1830 (see below), although he was vicar of the parish for thirty years (1817-1847). His successor, Julius Deedes, took a kinder approach to the subject when he wrote eight years later, just after his induction as vicar,

"It gives me great pleasure to find that the Parish of Marden is acting with so much consideration towards the large families of the Poor in consequence of the high price of provisions & I will gladly contribute my proportion according to my rating."

The parish provided flour for those in need between 1839 (the date of Stephen Walter's notice) and 1847. That period covered the time of agricultural distress and the high price of bread, before the Corn Laws were repealed in 1846.

38

Despite John Andrews' despairing comment in 1801, the amount of care, money and time devoted to the poor in the first half of the century is impressive. Poor Rates could be raised up to three times in a year. In 1835, for instance, Marden raised a two shilling rate, a two shillings and sixpence rate and a four shilling one (10p, 13p and 20p), which made a total for the year of just over £2,872. If translated into modern terms of money, it is doubtful whether the Welfare State could equal this for a parish of around 2,000 people. The recipients did not live easily, but life then, even for the affluent, was of a leaner kind than that which we demand today. The poor were expected, when they were able, to work hard to help themselves. But the records show a real spirit of concern and a sense of duty in the Overseers and their assistants towards their fellow villagers, only tempered by the very real problems caused by the depression in farming.

AN INVENTORY of goods belonging to Benjamin Spice, Pauper

Two pairs Tow Sheets
Two Blankets
One table cloth and 3 towels
A table
Chest of drawers
A small cupboard
3 chairs, one of which is an arm chair
One large Delft dish
5 plates and a poringer
Teapot
A white pint pot
2 spinning wheels
a Bible
a copper kettle and
warming pan
bellows
a Looking glass
a large Pitcher
a brass candlestick
3 china basins
3 cups and saucers
Patty pan
a pudding pan
one work basket, one
other ditto
one small silver teaspoon

(KAO P244 16/5)

Although Benjamin Spice was a pauper, his possessions do not suggest extreme poverty. His goods would have made his cottage quite a comfortable home. However, he may well have fallen into arrears with his rent or had become for some reason unable to earn enough money to keep himself without the help of the parish. Were the two spinning wheels a relic of the cloth trade?

Benjamin Spice died in October 1788.

Chapter Three

The Forces of Change

The Agricultural Riots of 1830

The 1820s were indeed a time of hardship for most people in the Weald. A Parliamentary report had mentioned an increase in paupery and that there were sixty men out of work in Marden (as in other parishes). As the decade progressed things did not improve, either for the low paid farm worker or for the tax and tithe ridden farmer.

The harvests of 1829 were disastrous. By the end of July at the Horsmonden Fair it was noted in the 'Maidstone Journal' that hops in the Weald " . . . were never worse than at present . . . " . Heavy rain and continual strong winds during August and September had reduced crops even further. The same newspaper reported that no hops at all were sold at the Cranbrook Michaelmas Fair – an unheard of event. At Maidstone it was the same: the 'Maidstone Journal' wrote in October 1829:

"If any proof were wanting of the poverty of the county and the alarming stagnation of trade, which everywhere prevails, that proof we should imagine must have been amply furnished by the state of business at our Fair . . . Scarcely a growth of hops, a drove of bullocks or horses changed owners. There were plenty of hop factors from London, but they showed not the least symptom of purchasing. In the Pleasure Fair we never remember having seen at Michaelmas such a paucity of exhibitions and other amusements."

Although the numbers in the Marden poor house remained fairly constant (about 40-55) during the year, the outdoor relief jumped from an average £100-£250 per month, to £751 in October 1829.

The winter which followed was a hard one; there was heavy snow in the Weald on Christmas Day and many plants and trees died during the cold weather. Added to this, the local corn stocks were low. The price of wheat was 65s. 2d. (£3.26) per quarter at the end of May, but this price benefited neither the poor nor the farmer whose harvest had been so miserable. The hops were again affected by pests and diseases. On 1st June the Overseers and churchwardens of several parishes, including Marden and Staplehurst, met at the Bull Inn, Maidstone, to discuss the distress of the parishes and decided to send a deputation to Parliament. In Ulcombe a high rate of 3s. 6d. (18p) had been granted for the poor, but Ulcombe's representative pointed out the hardship involved in paying it.

40

It is interesting at this distance from the events of 1830, to see how intertwined the needs and pleas for relief were. The farmers cited the suffering of the farm labourers in their own demand for the lowering of tithes and rents. Equally, the labourers were demanding of the clergy and landowners that they reduce the farmers' burdens so that they could raise farm wages. In Marden and the rest of the Weald the addition of the Hop Duty (payable on every pocket of hops) would make this unlikely. The Rector of East Farleigh was reported in the 'Maidstone Journal' to have returned a quarter of his tithes in February 1831. It is a pity we do not know whether the labourers did indeed benefit from this help to the farmers.

The Agricultural Riots began, in Kent, in the early autumn. It is likely that the prospect of yet another winter of low wages (compared with those of less than twenty years previously) and when in any case work would be scarcer than during the summer months, drove the men to form groups and make their demands for better pay. When the riots started there still appeared to be less of a division between master and man than might have been expected during the first half of the nineteenth century. When there was a large gathering of labourers (of about 300-400, according to the 'Maidstone Journal') at Linton Place at the beginning of November 1830, the local farmers and other men refused to be appointed special constables to deal with the situation; the army had to be called in. Six magistrates, Messrs T. Rider, J. Best, J. Jacobson, E Lushington, B. Duppa and W. Tyssen, together with the mayor and town clerk of Maidstone and a small detachment of cavalry confronted the rioters on Bottlescrew Hill, Boughton. Their spokesman, John Adams, was a journeyman bootmaker from Mr Marsh's shoe shop in Maidstone and he was supported by a fellow worker. The two were arrested, but were let off lightly, being required only to keep the peace in future. In fact John Adams was able to earn a good living: twenty-five or even thirty shillings a week were mentioned in the account of the trial.

The rioters dispersed for the time being, but the 'Maidstone Journal' said that on 6th November groups of labourers, mostly from Marden, Staplehurst and Frittenden, were meeting in the Cranbrook area, roaming about and calling on farmers " . . . who in the most instances relieved them either with refreshments or money . . . " . The report did not give any indication of violence or of damage.

The mood was slightly uglier in Goudhurst a few days later. On 15th November about a hundred labourers met there, led by William Standen, Stephen Eves and Richard Cutbush (termed by the 'Maidstone Journal' later as " . . . seditious and turbulent persons"). They flocked to Mr Springett's house, owner of the Great tithe and who also employed many men. Meanwhile, the Rev. Philip Le Geyt, vicar of Marden, who had been given word of the assembly, sent for the Dragoons who had just been despatched to Cranbrook by Sir Robert Peel. When the soldiers arrived the commander, Captain King, read the Riot Act and told the crowd to disperse. It is not clear how threatening the three ringleaders became, but they were arrested for assault, with sticks, on Le Geyt and Captain King.

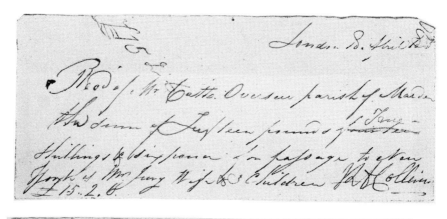

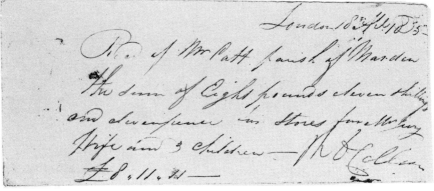

A bill to Mr Catt, Overseer of Marden, for the passages and stores for the Jury family, who were emigrating to the United States. 1835. KAOP 244 12/185

On the whole the Agricultural Riots were carried out with some moderation, although there were certain episodes where there was intent to do considerable damage. In a deposition taken at the East Kent Assizes, an Elham rioter said, "It was agreed that those who had no tools should stand out to watch and that we should hurt no-one if they came, nor give any foul language. After the machines were destroyed we all came away and when we got by the corner of the buildings we gave three cheers".

In fact there is little evidence of machine breaking in the Weald; that appears to have been confined on the whole to East Kent. Perhaps machines were not yet in favour in the Weald. There was an editorial comment in the 'Maidstone Journal' which suggested that not everyone was ready for the machine age. It said that threshing machines were wasteful and that crops were damaged by the

42

process. "It is surprising then that these instruments have not long since been laid aside as useless, which they no doubt would have been had not the distress of the times urged farmers to hurry their corn to market more quickly than the labourer with his flail could not (sic) enable them to do." There were threshing machines in a farm sale in Marden in 1851, but it is not known when they were brought in.

The usual damage done by the rioters in the Weald and the nearby districts was arson, though there is no record of any fire in Marden. Some fires which were reported to be of criminal origin turned out to be the usual burning of hop-bines. But certainly Earl Darnley of Cobham's estate was fired, a reminder, perhaps, of the passing of the Corn Laws in 1815. And one unfortunate at Ash was excused duty on the Grand Jury when arsonists set light to his property for a second time.

Often, however, the labourers were demanding a rise in wages: 2s. 3d. a day in winter and 2s. 6d. a day in summer (11p and 13p). Robert Price was the catalyst who set off the reactions of many groups. A deserter from the Navy, he was indicted for riot and misdemeanour at Stockbury, East Malling and Yalding during October and November. According to a deposition at the West Kent Quarter Sessions, however, he was disappointed at the small number of potential supporters he gathered at the last named village.

After the events of November the movement lost momentum and the labourers went back to the hard job of getting a living from the land. Their pay rose little before the last quarter of the century. Some men in the 1880s were still earning less than the desired 2s. 3d. or 2s. 6d.

Wheat prices continued to drop: top quality grain in 1831 started at 66 shillings and fell to 60 shillings by the end of the year, while poorer wheat (more common in the Weald) sold at 54 shillings in May, dropping to 44 shillings in December ('Maidstone Journal').

After allowing for exaggeration in newspapers and the traditional complaints of farmers, it does appear that there was little the farmer could do to improve the labourer's lot in the light of falling prices, high rents, tithes and taxes.

Christopher Wright in his 'Kent Through the Years' (1975) says that of the 129 rebels brought to trial after the riots, 25 were acquitted, 48 imprisoned, 52 transported to Australia and 4 executed.

Robert Price received four years hard labour; the three Goudhurst men were given eighteen months hard labour. None of the Marden men was charged.

Considering that it was only in the same year, 1830, that the crime of forgery ceased to carry the death penalty, the sentencing seems remarkably light. It was also effective for, apart from a few fires the following year (which may or may not have been directly related to agricultural wages), there was little further disturbance.

In January 1831 the editor of the 'Maidstone Journal' wrote with satisfaction that the government intended to keep the transported rioters apart from " . . . the more depraved and systematic class of convicts of a more different description . . . "

A water colour painting of Shepherds House and the Church, from the early nineteenth century.

Whether that was much comfort to the unfortunate fifty-two compulsory emigrants is not recorded.

The sympathy of authority and employers, however, did nothing to relieve the distress of the times. For several families the answer was emigration. The earliest mention in the records is in 1835 when some of the poor went to America. In 1838 at least two families from Marden were helped to go to New South Wales, Australia: Henry Newish, his wife and two children and also John Hunt with his wife and four children. John was the son of Richard Hunt, one of the Militia men mentioned above. In 1848 and 1849 other families were sent on their way. In March 1849 the Vestry noted that the aggregate amount of rates raised for the relief of the poor in the preceding three years had been £4,653, a great deal of money at a time when the New Poor Law Amendment Act might be thought to have reduced such high rates. In February 1849 the Vestry decided to borrow £100 to pay for emigration and six weeks later they were looking for another £49 for the same purpose. At least there was no further charge to the parish once the families were on board ship. Certainly there is a curious dip in the population between the census of 1831 (2,109) and that of 1841 (2,076). The number of baptisms dropped suddenly between 1838-1841. This may not necessarily mean fewer births, but it does suggest that. On the other hand there were fifty-six deaths in 1837, a higher rate than the average figure of thirty-five deaths, taken over a fifteen year period.

Despite the emigrating families of 1848 and 1849, Marden's population increased by 220 people by the time of the 1851 census (2,296). But of that figure, thirty-five per cent were born outside the village.

The Weald and Parliament

One of the by-products of the agricultural distress of the 1820s and 30s was the pressure for the reduction of the various taxes like tithes, hop-duty and the tax on malt. In November 1830 a speaker at a meeting held at The Royal Star Hotel, Maidstone said that this last tax prevented labourers " . . . from obtaining this nutriment as necessary for the support of their health and strength and compels them to drink water, which without supporting their ability for labour, has in many instances been followed by consequences destructive of health". Crocodile tears on the part of the farmers this may well have been, but the dangers of drinking water when typhoid and cholera were still fairly common in the country were probably not exaggerated.

In June 1830, just before the Agricultural Riots began, the Archbishop of Canterbury introduced the First Reading of a Bill which would change the payment of tithes on the amount of crops actually grown, to a system of putting a tax on land acres used or owned. If farmers had to pay church tithes at all – and this was the law for all, regardless of religious convictions – then it seemed more just to pay on acreage rather than on harvests. A tithe put on output discouraged the extra expense of raising production. No doubt some returns were falsified as far as the farmer thought he could deceive the calculating eye of the vicar. The amount of tax per acre would be decided in each parish by two Commissioners, one appointed by the local bishop and the other one voted in at a meeting of landowners. The Act took five years to define ready for the Statute Book and the Commissioners did not arrive in Marden until March 1841.

Meanwhile the farmers seized upon another popular idea of the period. electoral reform. Parliament consisted mostly of members who were gentlemen landowners or aristocrats; there was an opinion held by many that injustices and hardships in the country would not be removed until a body more in touch with the common people was elected. To achieve this, the system of electing members of Parliament would need to be changed.

A few days after the November Riots in the Weald in 1830, the farmers of Staplehurst wrote a petition to be presented to Parliament.

"We approach you, Honourable House; we tell you in language respectful yet plain, that our burdens are such that we can bear them no longer. We view with pain and dissatisfaction that extravagant expenditure both in Church and State, which although so often protested against by a suffering and starving nation, remains undiminished and we cannot see the last small portion of our capital torn from us and our dependent offspring, to be lavished on the useless sinecurist and the overpaid statesman, without praying most earnestly for that relief we candidly acknowledge we never expect to obtain, until by a consistent, practical Parliamentary Reform, your Honourable House is purged of its corrupt influence and contains in reality the Representatives of the People."

45

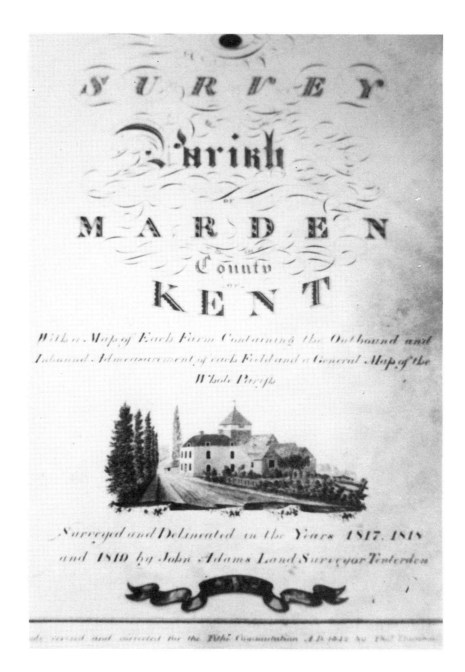

The frontispiece of the Marden book of estate maps.

46

There is no record that this fire breathing document ever reached the Commons, but the ideas were evidently shared by many.

In 1831 the 'Maidstone Journal' reflected and encouraged Reform fever when at last a Reform Bill was placed before the House of Commons. It was after all a moderate — even modest — Bill and most people could see the justice of eliminating rotten boroughs — except of course those Members who sat for these parcels of scantily inhabited land. In the Second Reading 302 Members voted 'Aye' and 301 'No'. It was pointed out in the 'Maidstone Journal' that of the 301 voting against the motion, thirty-eight Members represented twenty-three constituencies containing just eight hundred and fifty-eight electors. However, the Bill was defeated at the Committee stage and Parliament was dissolved shortly afterwards. It was clear that Reform was the main issue of the election in May 1831. Many areas had set up groups to agitate for the vote to be given to a larger proportion of people. In the Weald there was one called the 'Weald Friends of Reform' who supported two reforming candidates, T.L. Hodges and T. Rider. Their election was celebrated with a splendid (subscription) dinner at the 'George Hotel' at Cranbrook. Another Reform Bill was introduced during that year and after riots and another defeated government, the Bill finally went through on 4th June.

West and East Kent now sent two M.Ps each instead of two between them. A freeholder in Marden who owned property with a value of forty shillings retained his vote and was now joined by copy-holders and long lease holders whose land had a yearly value of £10. Tenant farmers and short lease holders who paid not less than fifty pounds in rent were also eligible. In 1835 only thirty people in Marden had property amounting to a rental value of fifty pounds or over. So the

Claim by Stephen Lefeaver of Stile Bridge to be placed on the Voters' List, after the Great Reform Act of 1832.

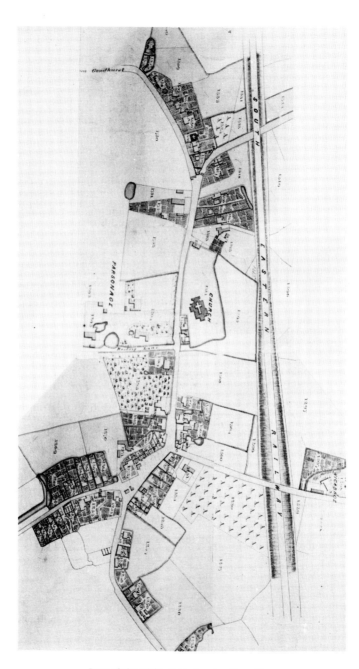

Part of the Tithe Map showing the railway.

48

number of voters who claimed to be put on the voters' register in July 1832: sixty-eight, does not seem a great improvement on the election of 1802, when forty-seven cast their vote, when one considers there were 449 more people in the parish. Of the sixty-eight, at least five people had their qualification questioned at the 1835 election. Even so, sixty-four people actually cast their votes – a high turnout by modern standards.

However, despite the limited increase in names on the Voters' register, the rule of the wealthy landowner in the House of Commons had begun to disintegrate and a few liberal ideas began to flow into Westminster.

The Coming of the Railway

One of the items to be considered by the newly elected Parliament of 1835 was the application of the South Eastern Railway Company for permission to make a railway line from London to Dover. The proposed system would radically alter the communications in the Weald, for it would provide for the first time an east-west transport link. The roads in the area had developed in a north-south direction by traditions probably dating back to the Roman roads and the early drove routes. Anyone who now attempts to drive from Marden to Dover, ignoring the A20, will know what a corkscrew procedure this is.

Earlier in this book it has been noted that the Wealden roads were often muddy and made trade difficult, particularly in winter. It was not easy to send stock and other produce to market, neither could farmers, builders and other tradesmen obtain bulky items, like bricks, fertilisers, timber or coal, either quickly or cheaply. The idea of a railway, unaffected by rain, gained much support. Surprisingly, a large part of the money subscribed to the new company came from the merchants of Liverpool and Manchester – presumably they had seen how successful such an undertaking might be. By 1836 over a hundred local people had invested over £200,000. A House of Commons Select Committee was set up to hear the evidence of those in favour of the railway and of those opposed to it.

Against the Bill were such groups as the inhabitants of Woolwich, the merchants and traders of Maidstone, rival railway companies like The London and Dover Railway Company and The London and Gravesend Railway Company and the Trustees and Creditors of the Tolls of the Road from Cranbrook to Maidstone. All these people feared, with justification, a loss of trade if the railway were built.

Maidstone, for hundreds of years a market for Wealden produce and an important staging post for the Weald trade with London, would be the most affected. Marden was especially close to the town. Many loads of timber, hops, corn and fruit were sent by waggon to Maidstone then down the Medway by hoy (a kind of barge), into the Thames estuary and so up to the city. J. Boys in his 'A General View of the Agriculture of the County of Kent' (1796) talked of the shipping of hops from the Weald and Maidstone districts " . . . creating in the

49

height of the season, an extraordinary scene of hurry and bustle in the streets and on the keys (sic) of Maidstone". He pointed out, however, that the journey by water needed two or three favourable winds. John Wilmshurst, a farmer and hop-merchant from Cranbrook, amplified this when he gave evidence at the Parliamentary Enquiry, saying that the journey took about thirty-three hours. In 1836 the freight charge from Maidstone to London for hops was fifteen shillings per ton, to be added to twelve or thirteen shillings waggon cost from Cranbrook to Maidstone. Marden's charge for hops would have been about twenty-two shillings a ton to London; those who sent fruit to the capital had to pay another three or four shillings for wharfage. If farmers sent their produce all the way by road, the cost was nearly twice as much as by water.

Transport of goods to the Weald was equally laborious and expensive, particularly for bulky freight like coal, chalk, shoddy, lime, timber and road mending materials. Farmers and merchants therefore tended to buy the minimum.

Samuel Johnson, a farmer from Goudhurst, was asked at the Enquiry:

Q. "Do you know any land more capable of improvement than this Weald of Kent?"

A. "I do not"

Q. "Would the improvement of the land occasion an increased labour for the working people?"

A. "No doubt."

Q. " . . . and give employment to the parish labourers?"

A. "Certainly."

Q. "And thereby prevent them from requiring relief to a certain extent?"

A. "Yes."

In 1836 that skilful piece of questioning must have influenced many who were responsible for raising the poor rates in their parishes.

The South Eastern Railway proposed a speed of 24 miles per hour from London to Tonbridge and 28 miles per hour from Tonbridge to Dover, compared with a land speed by coach of 8 miles per hour. As Maidstone had as yet no firm plans for a railway (though a branch line from Paddock Wood opened in 1844), it was suggested that the townspeople would go to Marden by road and then by train to London. This would, the committee were told, save Maidstonians one hour and thirty-six minutes of travelling − 2 hours 39 minutes by road and rail against 4 hours 30 minutes by coach to London. One wonders whether the rail enthusiasts had entered winter mud into these calculations.

Peter Sinclair, Superintendent of the Bolton, Leeds and Kerryon Railway was asked whether such extreme speed would harm passengers " . . . in taking away their respiration . . . " , but he assured them that everyone would be quite unconscious of the rate at which they were travelling.

The Company planned to build twenty bridges to accommodate Turnpike roads on the way to Dover as well as several bridges for smaller roads. Marden's Turnpike bridge was estimated to cost £1,223. 1s.; the old bridge over Pattenden Lane was put down for £915 and the little Wanshurst Green Arch whose solidity was demolished with such difficulty recently was entered in the estimate at £559.2s.

Within six years of the Enquiry date, 1842, Marden station opened for traffic. In May of that year the 'Maidstone Journal' published the following:

"In the excavation of the cutting for the railway at Marden, a splendid fossil elephant or mammoth (one tooth weighs over 20lbs) has been discovered 20 feet below the surface – this fact will be interesting to geologists as the organic remains of this animal has never before been found so low in the series as the Weald formation in which the cutting is supposed to be made, and appears to prove that the Marden hill is composed of a recent deposit above the Weald clay. A portion of the bones is in the possession of Mr Barlow, the resident engineer of the line at Tonbridge, who is endeavouring to collect the whole animal; but unfortunate(ly) several waggon loads containing the remains were thrown into the embankment by the workmen."

Sadly, nothing more was heard of Mr Barlow's mammoth.

The line from Redhill to Ashford opened in 1842, the stretch from Ashford to Folkestone in 1843 and the difficult piece on to Dover was finished in 1844. (The South Eastern Railway had running rights over the London to Brighton line from London to Redhill.)

It is not easy to assess what effect the railway had on Marden. Probably in the early days it might not have altered the village very much. There had always been an active exchange of people and news between the surrounding parishes and Maidstone. The 1840 Piggot directory, for example, shows that the post arrived in Marden from Maidstone at eight o'clock every morning – on foot – and that letters were sent into the town each evening at six. But now came the opportunity to travel to more places and at a much faster rate.

It is not possible to compare the numbers of people who moved into the village to live before the railway came, with those who settled there after 1842. Unfortunately the census of 1841 does not show birthplaces of the residents. However, there is quite a difference between the percentage of villagers born outside the parish in 1851 – 35% – and that of those born elsewhere in 1881 – 55.1%; more than half of Marden's residents were not native to the village.

The favoured villages for immigrants changed, too. In 1851, just nine years after the station opened, Goudhurst headed the list of birthplaces:

Origin of Marden Residents

1851		1881	
Goudhurst	82	Staplehurst	96
Staplehurst	71	Goudhurst	78
Yalding	63	Cranbrook	60
Cranbrook	40	Sussex	126
Sussex	70	Other counties	23
Other counties	20	London	22
London	1		

Strangely, Tonbridge residents were never keen to move to Marden: only 3 by 1851 and still only 10 by 1881. At the other end of the line, however, Headcorn increased its contribution to Marden numbers from 9 in 1851 to 32 in 1881. The popularity of Yalding as a population builder cannot be explained by the train, but the movement of tradespeople and professional men into the village must have been eased by the coming of the train.

It would be rash to say that the railway influenced the kind of crops that Marden and the rest of the Weald grew. It is often suggested that the growing of fruit responded to the facility of sending it to the London markets by rail. In the twentieth century this was probably true and even more so when the railway put on a special train for the carriage of farm produce. But it is difficult to know whether the enormous growth in the fruit industry at the end of the nineteenth century was due to the lure of London markets — and others more distant — or whether it was tied to the decline in hops and cereals.

However, a perishable crop like fruit certainly had expanding opportunities on the rail. It no longer had to rely on local markets for a quick, possibly unprofitable sale or to chance the damage inevitable in a long waggon and hoy journey, with the necessary frequent handling. It is interesting to see that the C.M. Fox group of farms in the eighties were using the train to transport fruit. There is little doubt, too, that the carriage of fertilisers, wood and other large requirements of farming, building, brewing, tool and machine making and other industries became easier and cheaper. These industries in turn were able to become more efficient and cost effective.

Chapter Four

Victorian Marden

Marden in 1851

By 1851, we have a reasonable idea of how the village looked. There were 2,292 people, of whom about a third, 732, were children aged ten years or under. Thirty burials are recorded for the year, which included eight infants of less than a year old.

Marden was still largely self supporting; there was a good spread of trades and shops which could supply most of the needs of the house and of agriculture — still Marden's biggest industry. Shoemaking was a popular alternative to farm work for there were four master boot and shoemakers and twelve journeymen in the parish. William Day at White Lyon House was a tailor and so was John Burnham, who also had a fourteen year old apprentice. Two straw bonnet makers and several dressmakers completed the clothing services offered by the village.

Three butchers supplied the meat and among the four grocers of Marden, William Jude combined his business with a post office (helped by his fourteen year old niece, Sarah Iggulden). Frederick Hill, churchwarden, had a drapery section in his grocer's store. In the Maidstone Road, Sophia and Caroline Southon, sisters, baked bread and cakes for all those who did not make their own.

Naturally in a farming community there were many craftsmen: William Parsons was a cooper, William Cleaver a farrier and there was also a saddler and a harness maker. Four wheelwrights worked in the village; one near Stile Bridge, two in the centre of the village and one on Winchet Hill. They all served the Turnpike road just as service stations are placed today to make the most trade out of motor traffic. They also did work for their farm and carriage customers. Carpentry jobs were carried out by three master carpenters and their four assistants; there were also two blacksmiths, several bricklayers, a master brick-maker and a thatcher.

Five carriers brought in the other needs of the parish (not covered by the train) and took out produce for sale, often on a smaller scale than that carried on by the rail or the farm waggon. It was useful, for instance, for the cottage garden crops which could be sold in the Maidstone market.

Several women were heads of businesses in 1851; mostly they were widows, keeping trades going with their sons, like Ann Stanley, blacksmith, who had three journeymen blacksmith sons. Susan Pain kept a grocer's shop, Susan

53

The Unicorn Inn

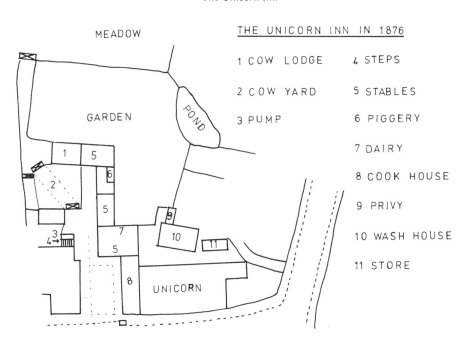

MEADOW

GARDEN

POND

THE UNICORN INN IN 1876

1 COW LODGE   4 STEPS

2 COW YARD   5 STABLES

3 PUMP   6 PIGGERY

7 DAIRY

8 COOK HOUSE

9 PRIVY

10 WASH HOUSE

11 STORE

Plain Farm Oast. Incised on wall of right hand kiln: S.D.1867.

Williams was a butcher, while Fanny Austen, Mary Osborne, Mary Hayes and Mary Leeds were all farmers in their own right.

In fact Marden had sixty-six farmers; James Day held the most land, at The Plain, with 472 acres and employed twenty-eight men. Some farmers combined two jobs: Stephen Lefeaver at the Stile Bridge Inn also had 190 acres and employed nine men. At 'The Unicorn', Thomas Day, brother of the tailor, was not only an inn-keeper, but farmed 95 acres.

One of the busiest parts of the parish must have been Mount Pleasant, where Henry Brown (styled 'gentleman' in the directories) and his wife, Adelaide, owned and ran a fruit plantation, employing twelve men, and also an earthenware pottery where another ten men worked. Just for good measure Henry Brown was a churchwarden, too.

William Hammond and his son ground corn for the village at Pattenden Mill; nearby at Gravel-Hole (Gravel-Pit), there was a tea dealer who came originally from Yalding. Indeed, several tradesmen, merchants and professional people had moved into the village (encouraged by the train?). There was Edward Kenward, a hop merchant from Sussex, who no doubt had an interest in the considerable hop production in the area. James Small from Surrey had set up as a timber broker; Doctor Robert Perry at Bridge House came from Exeter and had qualified in Glasgow. Edwin Boucher and his wife, who ran the National School, were

55

both originally from Gloucestershire; Richard Langton, who had the Classical and Commercial Academy at Shepherd's House, came from Norfolk.

There was a surprising amount of movement among farm workers, too. Of the 428 men who earned their living on the land in Marden in 1851 (excluding farmers and their sons), 132, just under a third, came from other parishes. Farmers tended to hire for a particular job or for a season rather than regular year round employment as we know it today, so travelling around was a way of getting a job.

Perhaps the most outstanding traveller of any group in the village was William Iggulden, one of the butchers, who was born in Marden, married a girl from Lancashire, had a daughter in Bangalore and was back in the parish with his family in 1851.

The most prosperous inhabitant of that year must have been the Rev. Julius Deedes, who occupied the very good living of Marden of £545.19s.2d. per year. On top of that (based on the 1841 survey) he received annually another £400 from the Extraordinary Tithe on hop acreage, making his stipend £945.19s.2d. This was a tremendous amount, especially compared with the lot of the farm worker whose annual wages totalled about £32 — if he were lucky enough to work a full year. No wonder the vicar could afford a nurse, a footman, three house servants and a governess from France. John Hedgecock, the Congregational minister, had one servant and boarded a ten year old scholar from Chatham.

Although 1851 was still nineteen years away from compulsory education, fifty-seven per cent of the children between five and fourteen years (310 children) were in a school of some sort. There were probably one or two dame schools to deal with this large number, in addition to the National School and the Classical and Commercial Academy. A few children like those of John Hooker, an agricultural manure agent, and the vicar's family had their lessons at home.

Two elderly residents of that year held official posts in Marden. John L. Noakes, now aged eighty, was still Parish Clerk, dealing with Vestry affairs and teaching as well. Thomas Botten carried out the not too arduous duties of Beadle, although he had passed his eighty-eighth birthday.

In the midst of all this industry how did Marden relax in 1851? One way was to play and watch cricket. Many years before a club had been formed at Stile Bridge; in 1829 Stephen Lefeaver was its enthusiastic captain and his family had always taken an active part in the team. In 1851 they started the season with nine new members, including Henry Hammond from the Mill whose father, William, had played in the team ten years before.

1851, too, was the year of the Great Exhibition at Crystal Palace; it was an advertisement of British trade and of the riches of the empire. The 'Maidstone Journal' was eloquent:

"This Exhibition is literally the greatest 'sight' in the World . . . We read in Arabian fables that magicians could place before enchanted spectators the visible treasures of the universe. These very treasures are now laid bodily at our feet."

Many local firms sent their employees to enjoy the Exhibition – and gave them the money to do so. No doubt the train from Marden contained a few passengers who were willing to pay the shilling (5p) entrance money to be 'enchanted'.

However, enjoying the treasures from Bengal, Constantinople and Berlin was one thing, but tolerating other people's beliefs was quite another. In 1829 Roman Catholics had at long last been given civil equality with the rest of the country. They could now take any office except that of Regent or Lord Chancellor (these two appointments were open to very few protestants anyway). But in an area like the Weald, with its long history of non-conformity, this was not a popular move. Marden and other parishes had done their best to prevent equality – fortunately with no success – by signing a petition condemning the passing of the Bill, which Sir Edward Knatchbull presented to the Commons. In 1851 the Pope created Catholic bishoprics in England, which once more stirred up anti-Rome feelings.

Thomas Oyler Beeman, a noted preacher from Cranbrook, gave a lecture at the Classical Academy in Marden on 'The Principles and Influence of Romanism'. At the end a resolution was passed that " . . . the meeting, believing the prevalence of Popery in any country to be destructive of its general wellbeing, consider it to be the duty of everyone to do all that he lawfully may to resist the progress of that system". Fortunately no opportunity for action seems to have presented itself to our forebears, who on the other hand gave such reluctant financial support with their tithes to the established church, which was presumably their strongest defence against Rome.

Another controversial issue was still present in 1851: electoral reform. For despite the passing of the 1832 Reform Act, only about one sixth of those men old enough to vote were legally entitled to do so. The 'Maidstone Journal' had forgotten its previous attack of reform fever and felt things had now gone far enough. Apparently the 'Daily News' had pressed for an extension of the vote to all householders and had suggested that to avoid the evils of bribery and threats to which the poorer electors would be more vulnerable, the secret ballot should be introduced. "Now this," thundered the editor of the 'Maidstone Journal', "we should have thought an excellent reason for declining to descend so low in the scale, but to keep as we are." No doubt he himself qualified for a vote.

Those without property qualifications in the countryside continued to be overlooked in parliamentary election lists until 1884. As late as 1881, only 77 Marden men voted out of a total population of 2,321 – just 13% of the men over the age of 20.

One last look at 1851 and it is linked with the new railway. In September a woman from Scotland was visiting her sister who lived at Hunton. While there, she became seriously ill and the sister wanted to contact her brother-in-law. A message was sent by telegraph from Marden station at eight o'clock in the morning to his home in Glasgow. Twenty-four hours later the husband was sitting at his wife's bedside in Hunton. Even ten years before he could not have managed it in such a short time.

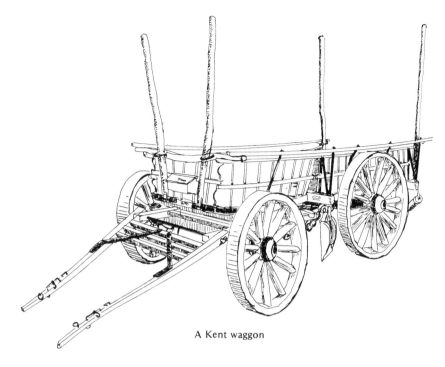

A Kent waggon

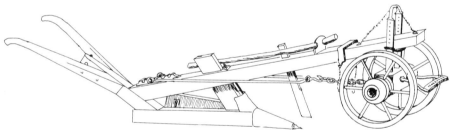

Kent wheel plough

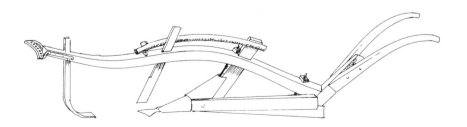

Kent foot plough

An engraving of a Kent turnwrest plough from Boys 'General View of Agriculture in the County of Kent', written in 1796.

The two new facilities in Marden, the train and the electric telegraph (by law available to everyone, not just railway staff), had certainly revolutionised communications. For in the same year, 1851, the undersea cable from Dover to Calais was completed and in theory anyone in the village could now exchange messages with Paris – technology every bit as wonderful as the treasures of the Great Exhibition.

Agriculture in the Second Half of the Nineteenth Century

In October 1851 Great Cheveney was sold and two weeks before a Live and Dead stock sale was held there. It gives us an idea of the kind of equipment and animals a three hundred acre farm had in the middle of the century.

"12 good draft Horses, 2 Colts and a well bred Nag Colt, 67 Kent Ewes, 62 Kent lambs, 30 Down (Southdown) Ewe tegs, 10 in Calf and Maiden Sussex Heifers, 7 Yearling Steers, 7 Calves, 9 Capital Sussex Milch Cows and 5 Welch Heifers in Calf, 2 Sows with Pigs, 26 Store Pigs and a Quantity of Poultry.

"2 broad wheel and 2 narrow wheel waggons, 3 tugs, 8 carts, 8 ploughs, a mole draining plough, 3 corn drills, harrows, rolls, brakes, 2 horse threshing machines, a hand ditto, cleaning machines, 2 sets of 4-horse harness, plough and other harness, hop-bins, bin-cloths and the usual oast tackle, with a numerous assortment of the smaller Farming implements.

"A portion of the useful Furniture in the Dwelling House, comprising tent and four-post bed-steads and Furniture and bedding, Chests of Drawers, Chairs, Tables, Carpets, a Pianoforte, a Baker's patent Mangle, dairy and brewing utensils and a Four Wheel Chaise and Harness."

The twelve horses may have made up three teams of four when the men were ploughing. The Weald used the heavy wooden Kent wheel plough or the slightly

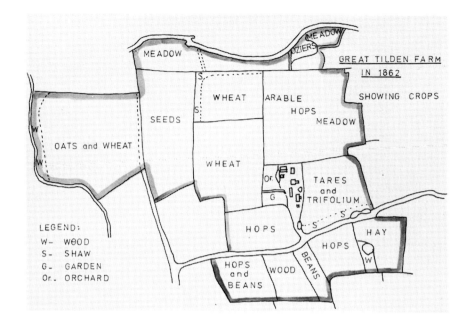

lighter foot plough, which had an iron foot instead of the large pair of wheels at the front. Iron ploughs, which were lighter than the two wooden Kent ploughs, were made from the middle of the nineteenth century onwards by Ransomes of Ipswich and Howards of Bedford, but they found little favour in Marden or the rest of the Weald. Nearly all the classes in the Marden, Staplehurst and Collier Street Agricultural Association Ploughing Match competitions were for wooden ploughs. From 1890 there was a class for iron ploughs, but until 1914, when the matches ceased, there were never more than two or three entries in that class each year.

Does this mean that the heavier ploughs, described by John Boys in his 'General View of Agriculture in the County of Kent' as long ago as 1796, ploughs which demanded at least four horses, a waggoner and a mate instead of the man and two horses required by the iron plough, were more suitable for the difficult Wealden soil? Or can it have been that Wealden farmers were more conservative than their counterparts elsewhere?

The harrows, too, were like those described by Boys: a strong wooden frame which was fitted with iron teeth. These survived even longer, well into the 1930s and a few may still be lurking at the back of farm buildings today.

The mention of the mole plough was rather unusual for the time; it was a more modern development and a short term answer to the perpetual problem of the Wealden high water table.

A tug was a kind of waggon but the sides were not boarded, while the narrow wheel and broad wheel waggons mentioned in the sale are interesting because they would have been charged different rates when they ran on the Turnpike road (which adjoined Great Cheveney). Narrow wheeled waggons had to pay an extra penny because they cut up the road more than the broad wheel ones.

Machines were beginning to figure more generally in farming from the middle of the century onwards. Garrett's Medway Ironworks, a branch of Garrett's of Leiston, advertised their new reaping machine with the rash statement that it was "almost impossible to put out of repair". But there does not appear to have been much movement towards this machine until the 1880s. It would be useful to know, too, whether the threshing machines listed in the sale catalogue were in the village during the 1830 Agricultural Riots, but there is no record. However, the mobile threshing unit was not a practical idea until the advent of the steam engines and these did not arrive in Marden until the last quarter of the century. The 1881 census shows Alfred and Frederick Foreman, Traction Engine and Machine Proprietors; they lived at the 'White Cottage' (next to Blue House) and they used their machine for threshing. Henry Britcher of Beech Farm was one of their customers. They probably also used the machine for haulage; certainly the steam engine at Dairy Farm (owned by C.M. Fox) pulled loads in the 1880s, particularly stone from the quarry Fox owned at Boughton Monchelsea. At the turn of the century he had forty clients to whom his drivers took the steam driven threshing tackle.

The Public Record Office at Kew stores records of crops which were grown in each parish; these start from 1867. The figures show the spread of livestock and plant there was in the nineteenth century and they also indicate the fluctuations of such produce.

As the Great Cheveney sale demonstrated, most farms had sheep, cattle, pigs, poultry and arable crops: wheat, oats, barley, beans and peas. Unfortunately the records do not show orchard acreage for 1867, but it was still relatively low in 1881 (although nearly three times the amount grown in 1841) at 334 acres.

The difference of wheat acreage between 1867 and 1901 reflects the severe depression that arable farming went through in the last twenty years or so of the nineteenth century. By that time the American wheat prairies were growing great quantities of cereals which were shipped to Europe freely, partly because shipping freight charges came down in price. In 1867 Marden grew wheat on 1007 acres; by 1901 this was lowered to 298 acres. Barley was never a large crop in Marden so the national decrease did not make much difference. Oat yields did not fall so much, presumably because a high proportion was grown for farm animals.

In many other areas of the country, the numbers of cattle, sheep and pigs rose as the cereal trade collapsed. Interestingly the difference was not so marked in Marden as it was to be in the depression following the first world war. In 1867 there were 539 cattle, 795 in 1881 and down again to 559 in 1901. Sheep numbers rose gently but steadily from 3072 ewes in 1867 to 3766 in 1901.

A crop of apples at Dairy Farm about 1900. Compare the height of trees with those planted today.

Fruit and hop machinery available in the 1920s. An advertisement by W. Weeks and Son of Maidstone.

However, Marden's farming did not depend on cereals and stock. As the wheat market disintegrated, the parish initially planted more hops, but later, increasingly more fruit. These tactics probably kept its farming in better economic order than that of many other parts of the country. In the years following 1881, which was about the last 'good' farming year for some time, orchard acres more than doubled, totalling 788 acres in 1901.

Account books of some Marden farms from 1886 to 1890 show, as already noted, how wide a spread of crop enterprises there were at that period. The cereals given are wheat, oats, peas, beans and a little rye, barley and tares (a vetch fodder crop). To feed the stock they also grew grass (for hay), clover, trifolium, mangold wurzel, swedes and turnips. They also raised cabbages, potatoes and hops; the fruit was equally extensive: apples, pears, plums, damsons, currants and strawberries. Fruit sold quite well. At Covent Garden in 1881 apples made 7s. to 15s. (35p to 75p) a bushel (40lbs). That money was the range of pay for a boy and a man working a full week on the farm. Cabbages sold at 2s. to 4s. per dozen (10p to 20p), new potatoes: 9d. to 1s.6d. (4p to 8p), turnips 4d. to 6d. a bunch (2p to 3p).

One factor in the increased fruit and hop production, apart from the decline in cereals, was that for the first time growers were better able to control the pests and diseases which plagued hop gardens and orchards in earlier days. In 1849 for instance, national production of hops had been 146,668 hundredweights grown on nearly 43,000 acres. Five years later, in 1854, the total produced was only just over 88,000 hundredweights on 54,000 acres. The hop-damson aphid, red spider and mould could all severely damage a hop-garden, while orchards had similar problems. Henry Britcher's accounts for Beech Farm in the 1890s show that he frequently applied sulphur, a specific against mould on hops. Soft soap and Quassia chips, too, were favoured though not particularly effective hop insecticides. The first hand spraying machine in Marden was one made by Warners of London in 1893 and owned by Thomas Honess of Great Cheveney. This beautifully preserved machine is still in working order and holds sixteen gallons of wash.

Farmers used plenty of organic manure. Account books record the use of lime, mould (presumably leaf-mould), shoddy, feathers, fur waste, bird manure, rags and of course the home produced dung from the cattle yards. The large work-forces on the farms of that time were kept very busy dealing with the fetching and spreading of all these fertilisers, in addition to all the normal planting, cultivating and harvesting of the various crops.

It is easy to forget in these days of high mechanisation on the land just how much human and animal labour was involved in feeding the nation a hundred years ago. The following is a record of a year's work at a group of farms in Marden during the year 1886/7. The farms, which included Dairy, Tanhouse, Widehurst and Folly farms belonged to Charles Montague Fox, or C.M. Fox as the company later became known. He began life as a poor London boy who started a successful career by selling pillows and then founded a feather bed

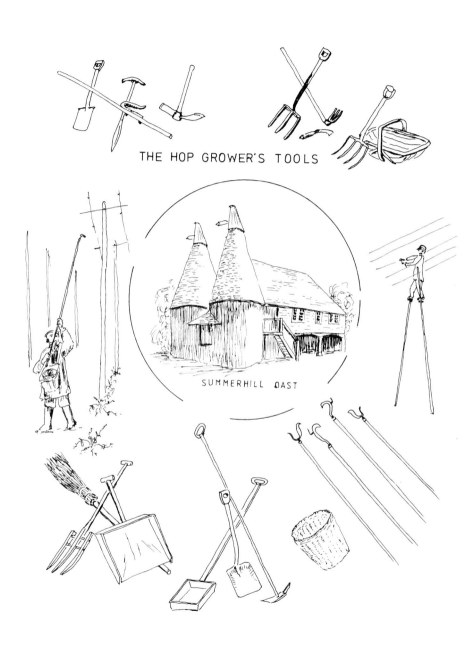

THE HOP GROWER'S TOOLS

SUMMERHILL OAST

Dairy Farm about 1900

factory. In time he bought the farms in Marden and was much respected by his employees and their families. One or two people still remember how he made sure that all his employees in Marden and London had a good piece of home killed beef for Christmas and that he gave the residents of Chainhurst a chapel.

A Year on the Farm: an analysis of farm work month by month.
OCTOBER 1886
  Apple picking, packing, carting fruit to Marden station, mending ladders.
  Striking up hop gardens (into ridges), grubbing hops and carting roots, carrying bines, pulling poles, carrying and stacking poles, spreading feathers (as manure)
  Ploughing, harrowing, sowing and drilling wheat, picking up couch.
  Pulling, carting and clamping wurzel.
  Attending to mare.
  Carting cattle cake from Maidstone, carting hay.
  Six men all day at Maidstone Fair, October 10th. (Taking or fetching stock probably).

65

NOVEMBER 1886

Apple picking (first week only), apple packing and hauling to station.

Digging holes for fruit trees, cutting trees, planting trees, planting cobnut trees, grubbing currants and whitewashing trees.

Pulling, carting and stacking poles, chopping poles (old ones no longer useful in the hop garden), cording poles, carting bines and carting dung.

Ploughing and sowing wheat, harrowing.

Clamping wurzel, lifting and carting swedes and threshing peas.

Breaking stones, manure spreading, chopping rags and bags (for fertiliser)

Hauling brushwood, ashes from Tovil (probably from the paper mills), feathers from the station.

Carting peas to Maidstone.

DECEMBER 1886

Tree cutting, tying, tying up cuttings, hoeing round damson trees, whitewashing trees, stumping trees.

Digging strawberries, grubbing strawberries.

Packing fruit and carting to station.

Carting hop-bines, spreading shoddy and feathers, carting dung and spreading mould, grubbing hops, carting hop-roots, stacking hop-poles and chopping poles.

Carting swedes.

Threshing wheat, oats, barley, beans and cleaning wheat.

Oiling harness.

Pig killing. Picking fowls and ducks.

Wood cutting, hedge brushing, ditching, levelling hassock.

Crushing beans, sorting potatoes, chaff cutting.

Thatching a stack, cleaving fencing spiles, tanking (tarring spiles and poles), scraping road and cutting bags.

Ferreting and rabbit shooting.

Hauling litter, hay, ditchings.

Fetching wood, straw, cattle cake from station, coal from Marden yard.

Taking straw to Hunton, wheat to the mill, feed to sheep.

Apples to London, two men two days.

JANUARY 1887

Cutting trees, planting trees, cutting currants and gooseberries, digging gooseberries, digging plantation.

Hop digging.

Ploughing.

Pulling turnips, cutting cabbage.

Spreading dung, shoddy, feathers.

Digging up quick (hedge), planting quick, planting willows, hedge brushing.

Making sticks (probably packing sticks for fruit baskets), wood cutting, tanking, cleaving fence spiles, moving gates, building a lodge, mending fence and gates.

Cutting and spreading bags and rags.

Cutting out hay.

Making a lawn (probably for the house).

Carting brush, dung, poles, gates, hay, wirework bats, litter, clearing from river.

Carting feed to sheep.

Wheat to station, hops to station, fruit to station, potatoes to station.

Fetching bats, bricks, ashes, lime, fruit trees from Maidstone and Brenchley.

FEBRUARY 1887

Packing apples, cutting trees, whitewashing trees, tying trees, tying cuttings digging plantations, making and putting on tree guards.

Ploughing hops, hop-digging, hop-dressing.

Ploughing, sowing and harrowing peas and oats, drilling and harrowing beans.

Spreading dung, mould, shoddy, fur waste and feathers.

Driving sheep, dagging sheep (trimming hind quarters ready for lambing).

Hedge brushing, wood cutting, cleaving fencing, making a foot for the stack, ditching.

To fair with a horse.

Cutting bean haulm, chopping bags.

Carting straw, feed to sheep. Coal, tiles, timber and sand from the station.

MARCH 1887

Cutting trees, tying trees, stumping trees, whitewashing trees, digging plantations, levelling plantations, packing fruit.

Ploughing and striking up hops, hop dressing, hop poling, cultivating with nidget. (See illustration)

Ploughing, drilling white peas, drilling barley, harrowing, broadshare for wurzel.

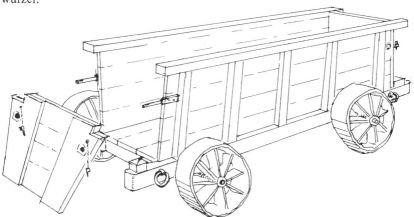

An Alley Bodge or Dung Dolly, used for taking manure up the narrow hop alleys.

Dredging, rolling wheat and harrowing it.

Preparing potato ground, striking up potato rows, planting potatoes.

Carrying in charcoal, laying turf, crushing beans, spreading feathers, dung, mould.

Filling in a ditch.

Cleaving fencing, wood cutting, hedge brushing, planting willows, tanking, hedge gapping.

Cutting chaff.

Chopping bags, sorting potatoes.

Spreading manure, carting hop roots, poles, brush, sand, mould, gates, feed to sheep, ashes from Tovil, cattle cake from Maidstone.

Fruit and potatoes to station.

APRIL 1887

Levelling plantation, stumping trees, nidgeting plantation, hoeing strawberries.

Hop dressing, poling, gapping up hop hills, priming hops (sprinkling a little fertiliser round each plant), poling the lee row (a row of hops on the headland of the hop garden which acted as a wind break), setting poles right.

Sowing oats, rolling and dredging meadows, harrowing wheat, oats, fallow.

Rolling wheat, oats, peas, trifolium.

Planting potatoes, drilling wurzel.

Sowing manure, bird manure.

Cleaving fencing, fencing, digging hedge, cutting down and grubbing hedge.

Breaking bones, bagging manure, chopping bags, mending fencing, filling ditch, hedge brushing.

Hoeing trifolium, burning couch.

Carting litter, ashes, wurzel, manure, feathers and fur waste.

Feed to sheep.

Carting bricks, poles, cattlecake and manure from station, ashes from Tovil, gates from Staplehurst.

MAY 1887

Hoeing plantation, hoeing round trees, liming trees, nidgeting plantation, picking off blooms.

Nidgeting, priming hops, setting poles right, hop tying (women), hop chopping.

Rolling and harrowing barley, rolling oats.

Rolling and harrowing for wurzel, harrowing beans, fallow, ploughing, braking peas, dredging.

Spreading feathers, hoeing thistles, hoeing wheat, hoeing beans, hoeing hedge.

Cleaving fencing, chopping bags, stripping pea sticks, digging post holes, putting in posts.

Carting ashes from Tovil, maize from Maidstone, cattle cake from Maidstone, corn to Staplehurst, delivering wheat.

Fetching bird manure, carting dung, feathers, ditchings, wurzel.

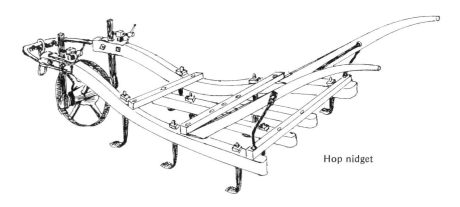

Hop nidget

JUNE 1887

Hoeing plantation, hoeing round trees.

Nidgeting hops, chopping hops, hop tying, priming hops, hoeing hops.

Ploughing, drilling wurzel, rolling, harrowing, drilling potatoes, earthing potatoes, braking wurzel, liming turnips.

Cutting trifolium, turning trifolium, mowing hay, mowing seeds, haying.

Hoeing peas, beans, wurzel, potatoes, oats.

Laying in drain, ditching.

Sheep shearing.

Fencing, hedge brushing, cleaving roots, tarring buildings, levelling road, chopping bags, mending sacks (women).

Stacking hay, pulling stack.

Carting tar from Maidstone, gates from Coxheath, lime from Bluebell Hill.

JULY 1887

Hoeing plantation, brutting trees, cutting down trees, grubbing trees, gathering cherries, packing fruit.

Nidgeting hops, hoeing hops, earthing up hops, sulphuring hops.

Ploughing, rolling, harrowing.

Mowing, turning hay, stacking hay.

Braking wurzel and turnips.

Planting wurzel, thinning wurzel, sowing turnips, hoeing swedes, hoeing potatoes, digging potatoes.

Cutting peas, tares, (a vetch fodder crop), turning peas and tares.

Mowing nettles and thistles, cutting and turning pea haulm.

Picking peas, watering strawberries.

Pegging tiles, cleaning engine (traction), laying pipes in drain.

Marking and driving sheep.

Pulling thatch off barn, pulling down barn.

Carrying hay, brushwood. Cattle cake and sulphur from Maidstone.

Fruit and peas to the station.

69

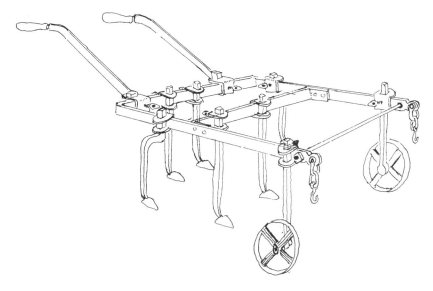

Worcester shim

SATURDAY 30th JULY 1887
Beanfeast for everybody. (This was probably for the Queen's Jubilee. She was proclaimed in Cranbrook on 31st July 1837, although she actually became queen on 20th June of that year.)

AUGUST 1887
Packing fruit, gathering apples, gathering plums, hoeing plantation.

Sulphuring hops, nidgeting hops, hoeing hops, cleaning hopper huts, whitewashing hopper huts, putting in bin cloths, cleaning oast, clearing barn (probably for the filled hop pockets).

Cutting wheat, oats, barley, beans. Ploughing.

Threshing tares, threshing, cleaning wheat and oats, harrowing for trefoil.

Carrying peas, beans, tares, wheat, oats, barley, beans.

Hoeing swedes, potato digging.

Tiles on barn, emptying well, cleaning knives, moving gates, dipping sheep.

Stacking wheat, barley, oats, beans, trimming stack, thatching stack. Loading wheat.

Fetching water.

Fruit and beans to station, tares to Staplehurst, wheat to Loose.

Sulphur and cattle cake from Maidstone.

70

Hop-picking at Dairy Farm about 1900. The hops are growing on pole work.

SEPTEMBER 1887

Gathering plums, damsons, pears, apples. Picking up apples and plums, packing apples, making packing sticks, bagging apples.

Striking up hops, putting down hairs (the horse hair floors in the oast kilns on which the hops were laid to dry). Measuring hops, drying hops, pulling poles, clearing old poles.

Hoppers to Marden (to the station at the end of hop picking), carrying in hop bins, washing bin cloths.

Ploughing for rye, harrowing trifolium, sowing and harrowing rye and tares.

Hoeing swedes, minding sheep, potato digging, picking up, sorting and clamping potatoes, furrowing and earthing celery.

Colt breaking, droving sheep.

Fetching coal. Taking wheat to Loose, hops and fruit to the station.

Fetching water. To Flimwell for goods and cow. To Maidstone with a pig. Feathers from the station.

Dairy Farm: Hop picking from 29th August to 23rd September.

C.M. Fox evidently made great use of the station; all his fruit in the year went by rail except one load which two men took to London in December.

71

Hop picking at Hartridge Farm, Thomas Judd (with measuring basket) about 1894/5. Son Arthur Judd is holding the poke.

Wages Account for week ending 19th August 1887

	No. of days	@ per day	Cash on acc.	£	s	d
Wm. Watts					15	0
A. Watts					9	0
Wm. Watts Jnr.					12	0
T. Winter					15	0
S. Reader					14	0
R. Osborne					10	0
C. Tolhurst					14	0
W. Brooks			15/-	1	6	0
L. Reader	6	3/-			18	0
A. Rhoads	4	2/2			8	8
C. Foster	6	2/2			13	0
R. Taylor	5½	2/2			11	0
W. Mercer	2½	2/2			5	5
G. Jenkins Snr.	2½	2/2	20/-	1	5	5
W. Brooks Snr.	3	2/2	4/-		10	6
A. Collins	5½	2/-			11	0
G. Atkinson	3	2/2	6/-		12	6
W. Tolhurst	5½	2/-			11	0
T. Fancett	5½	2/-			11	0
G. Goad	5	1/3			6	3
G. Jenkins Jnr.	1½	1/3			1	10½
A. Jenkins	5½	9d.			4	1½
G. Jolly (Carpenter)	6	3/4		1	0	0

72

Hop picking at Hartridge Farm, Thomas Judd (with beard), about 1894/5. These hops are growing on pole work, note how the pole has been pulled up and laid along the top of the bin.

A. Hunt (Bricklayer)		5	4/-		1	0	0
W. Taylor		3½	2/2			7	7
J. Taylor		5½	2/-			11	0
					16	4	3
Rents: A. Rhoads	2/2	L. Reader	2/6				
C. Foster	2/6	W. Taylor	2/0				
W. Mercer	2/6		11/8	Rents		11	8
					15	12	7

These accounts show that, despite the Riots of 1830, few people actually earned the desired 2s.6d. per day even fifty years later. William Watts Snr. was a waggoner and earned a regular 2s.6d. a day all the year round. L. Reader was paid 2/4 for most of the year in 1887, but in the summer, between April and the end of September, his rate went up to 3/- per day. There was no pay for sickness: G. Jenkins Jnr was ill for three days in the August week, so his pay (boy's) for the week was only 1s.10½d. (9p).

Mrs Bessie Hickmott's father, Robert Osborne, was earning 10s a week (50p) in 1887. By 1904 he was stockman and earned 2s.10d. all the year round. For other men in that year, top summer pay was 3s.2d. and 2s.9d. in winter, with threshing – a hard and dirty job – 3s. a day.

Mrs Hickmott says that life was not easy for families in those days. "We used to buy the skimmed milk – we couldn't afford the fresh." Out of his seventeen shillings a week, too, Robert Osborne gave money to his parents. "When they

Stile Bridge Farm Oast. This was the kind of building used for drying hops before the traditional (but later) shape of oast house had evolved. The hops picked in illustrations 38 and 39 were dried on this oast.

finally got an old age pension of seven shillings and sixpence a week (37p) they thought they were in clover." The young Bessie Osborne was glad of the good soup and bread sold for ½d. to the children of Marden school during January and February every year.

It was not until the 1914-1918 war that wages on farms rose as demand for home grown food increased and the supply of able bodied men in agriculture diminished.

One last look at the hop garden and oast house; by the end of the century they were both very different from those which the Rev. John Andrews saw in 1801. In the hop gardens, an overhead system of wirework strung with coir yarn was beginning to replace the hop poles. The older varieties of hops were also changing. Richard Fuggle of Brenchley raised the variety which was named after him; the Fuggle hop gained much favour in the Weald and continued to be the mainstay of Marden hop gardens for the next fifty years.

In the oast houses, a mechanical press removed the need for a man, usually the most junior member of the crew, to stand in a suspended pocket while the dried hops were rained down upon him (with a scuppet) into the pocket, so that he could press the hops with his feet.

Even the oasts themselves were not the same; they were bigger, the kilns taller and many of them were now fuelled with high grade anthracite coal (brought by rail) instead of with charcoal. Charcoal was still used, but only to start the fires off. Most of the present sixty-three oast houses (or remains) of Marden were built in the second half of the century.

Chapter Five

Nineteenth Century Vicars

It is to be expected that a hundred years of vicars would produce a group of vary-ing characters and in Marden's incumbents during the nineteenth century this is certainly true. It is difficult to give an accurate opinion of their temperaments, since village memory only extends as far as Thomas Arnold Carr (1882-1906). However, their written comments and their actions can in some way show us what they were like.

The longest serving vicar living in the nineteenth century was the Rev. John Andrews LLB JP (1766-1811). There is little doubt that he was autocratic: possibly the combination of his position as vicar, magistrate and a protegé of the Duke of Dorset made this inevitable. His unsuccessful attempt to manipulate the election of his choice for church warden has already been noted. In the following year he again clashed with the Vestry (led by the popularly elected People's Warden, John Burr) when, as was the custom, the Vestry appointed the Parish Physician. It had chosen Jonathon Monckton, son of the previous vicar. Andrews and his supporters said that a woman in the poor house had complained that Jonathon Monckton had been guilty of " . . . indecent and wicked behaviour" towards her, of which she was willing to swear on oath. The vicar's choice was William Hunt of Goudhurst, whom he and the other church warden also appointed. However, his contract was allowed to lapse and the Vestry's man, Monckton, became and remained Parish Physician for " . . . upwards of forty years . . . " as his memorial tablet in the North chapel in church shows.

Dominant though he may have been, there was possibly some quality in Andrews, a fair-mindedness, perhaps, not rooted in weakness, which allowed the village to defy him. There were few countries in Europe at that time, 1775, where such behaviour against the church would have been tolerated.

The records show Andrews to have been busily involved in looking after his flock. Despite his despair at the high Poor Rate in 1801, it was only after his death in 1811 that the parish found it was paying more than its neighbours to the poor – and thereafter reduced the Relief. As a magistrate Andrews may well have known the other rates, for although he might chide his parishioners, he gives an impression that he would not allow them to suffer.

For a Church of England minister, Andrews was unusual. He had presumably strong protestant ideas, which in 1794 led to his licensing a house for non-conformist ministers to preach the gospel: the Rev. E. Ralph of Maidstone, the

The Vicarage until the 1960s. The upper storey has since been removed. Philip Le Geyt was the first vicar to live here.

Rev. S. Beaufoy of Sutton Valence and the Rev. Josiah Moss and the Rev. Matthias Wilkes of Whitefields Tabernacle, London, were among those who visited. Later on, Joseph Clout, a Marden man, gave a chapel building which formed the beginning of the Congregational Church, with the Rev. H.L. Popplewell as minister. A friendly arrangement grew up, whereby the village went to the parish church for the morning service and sermon with Andrews. There was an afternoon service in the Congregational church and in the evening the vicar's wife and sometimes the vicar himself went to hear the minister preach.

As the Congregational church grew, the vicar initiated the buying by public subscription of ground adjoining and a new, bigger church was built. The old one was used to make a house for the minister. At his death, Andrews left £200 to be invested and the proceeds were to be given to the Congregational church together with his library of books.

After Andrews the next incumbent was Frederick Manners-Sutton, who must have been a shock to the parish. A nephew of the Archbishop of the same name, Manners-Sutton (1811-1817) was a noted pluralist and consequently an absentee vicar. Three days after being presented to the living of Marden he became vicar of Preston by Faversham and less than a year later he was rector of Tunstall. There can be few who regretted his departure in 1817.

In that year Philip Le Geyt (1817-1847) arrived in Marden. Although he was vicar for thirty years there are no stories handed down – possibly a sign that no-one cared enough about him to preserve any. The only two records of him, connected with the poor and the Agricultural Riots in Goudhurst, suggest that he may have lacked sympathy for at least some of his parishioners.

He had difficulty in getting the Church Rate (for general upkeep of the church) passed, but this happened also to his successors. It is possibly significant, however, that the next vicar, Julius Deedes MA, raised a threepenny rate in his first year with a unanimous vote in the Vestry.

Deedes (1847-1880) must have been a popular man, for, two years after his induction, the Archdeacon Benjamin Harrison approved new pews which were put into the church to cope with the growing congregation. After his death, too, the village gave the church the present pulpit, in his memory.

In 1854 the Vestry again refused to raise a Church Rate. Deedes then used his own money to make some alterations and to provide yet more pews. He had the pulpit moved (on the Archdeacon's suggestion) to the spot the later one occupies today and had new pews made in the gap which was left.

By 1871 when the Archdeacon again Visited there was much work to approve. Despite wrangles over the Church Rate and complaints that the valuation list was wrongly assessed, many repairs and additions had been made during Deedes' ministry, including a new Communion table and a new barrel organ in the west gallery. The windows in the south aisle had been 'restored' and were described by Glynne in his 'Churches of Kent' (1877) as "vilely mutilated, and some dormer windows inserted in the roof . . . " It is not clear when the dormer windows were built, although it sounds as though they were of recent making in 1877. We cannot judge the fitness of these developments since they were later removed, but Deedes' concern and care for the church must be appreciated.

Between 1880 and 1882, William Benham B.D. occupied the living. He was the Hampshire born son of a working man who attracted the attention of Archdeacon Bayley while he was a pupil at the local National school. Benham made good use of this patronage: he gained a first class honours degree at King's College, London, became a professor of modern history and was later appointed to preach regularly in Canterbury Cathedral. Life in Marden must have lacked further challenge, for two years was enough for him. However, he was busy while in the parish; he managed to build a new school room and, more remarkably, he persuaded William Walter to sell part of his orchard, which adjoined the church, for much needed burial ground. The Vestry had been trying to buy the land for the previous seven years.

Thomas Arnold Carr (1882-1906) replaced Benham; he had for twenty years been vicar of Cranbrook. He, like Deedes and Andrews before him, was very much involved in the life of his parishioners. Like Andrews, too, he was autocratic. The boys of the village were required to salute him whenever they met him in the street and the girls had to curtsey. One day he went to the school and said: "Some of you children are forgetting your manners and are not paying

The Church before the erection of the ragstone wall and the removal of the ivy, but after the erection of the vestry in 1887.

proper respect to your superiors. There is a product for sale in the shops called 'Jacob's Oil'; tell your parents to buy a bottle and rub your knees with it!"

However, Carr and his family were a driving force in the church. When they arrived there were fifty-three children in the Sunday School; by the time they left twenty-four years later there were four Sunday Schools and two hundred and fifty children on roll – at the National Schools, Marden Beech, Chainhurst and the Milebush.

Under his eye, too, flourished children's services, Bible classes, working parties for girls, mothers' meetings, Girls' Friendly Society (with a library attached), a branch of the Band of Hope, night schools, and Reading Rooms for adults at No. 1 Howland Road which were kept supplied with books and games.

Carr himself paid for the robing of the church choir with cassocks and surplices ready for the Easter services in 1883. He persuaded the village to buy a new harmonium for Chainhurst so that the old one could go to the Milebush school when it opened in March 1884. He also started the parish magazine which contained not only church news, but other essentials like school inspection reports and batting averages of the Marden cricket team. Carr's son, William Arnold, edited the magazine. This is his account of the Sunday School Treat, held on 22nd July 1884:

"At half past two the Marden Band began to play selections of Music while the children were taking their allotted places. Shortly afterwards the Church Bells struck up a merry chime, rung by some of the elder boys of the School,

78

and the Procession headed by the Band filed out of the school enclosure, each section having its distinctive banner; one representing the Good Shepherd led the way, followed by the boys and girls of the Bible Classes. Then came the children attending the Parish Church Schools with the members of the Band of Hope in their midst. These were in their turn, followed by the Infants who carried smaller flags and seemed much delighted with their burdens. The children attending the Chainhurst, Marden Beech and Mile Bush Mission Schools brought up the rear. The total number of children in the Procession was 214. After a short and bright service in the Church, the Procession re-formed and marched to the Vicarage meadow, where Cricket, Swings, Races and other amusements were thoroughly entered into and enjoyed by all. A bountiful tea was done ample justice to by the children, who shewed their appreciation of the kindness of the Vicar and Mrs Carr, to whose generosity the Treat was entirely due, by giving three hearty cheers before leaving."

This account seems to sum up Carr's ministry: benevolent, well ordered — but everybody knowing his or her correct place.

Thomas Carr's son, William, was also a popular figure. Known to the village as 'Mr Billy', he was ordained in 1900 and became his father's curate until his father's retirement, when he went as curate to Hove.

One of the more controversial episodes Thomas Carr had to deal with was the proposed restoration of the church. In 1883, the architect, T.G. Jackson of London, suggested removing the galleries, the dormer windows, the old high pews in the nave and the false deal roof which had been put up in the middle of the eighteenth century. He proposed to lower the whole floor of the nave and the aisles and put in open pews in the nave and the choir. He wanted to copy the tracery of the fourteenth century window in the north east of the church in making new windows in the south aisle and one in the north aisle. He planned to build a vestry on the ruins of a former building to the south of the tower. The heating would be supplied by two Porrit stoves under the floor.

Outside, he decided the existing stucco should go, the masonry be repointed and an open gutter be constructed around the whole of the church, to help dispose of rain water from the roof. Lastly he wanted to take away the 'ugly' snuffer on the tower and replace it with a wooden spire covered with shingles.

An appeal was launched, for the cost was estimated at £2,600 to £2,700. F.S.W. Cornwallis, owner of Linton Place and of several thousand acres of Marden gave £250 to set the scheme going.

All did not go smoothly, however, for Thackeray Turner of the vigilant Society for the Protection of Ancient Buildings (still very active and known more familiarly as SPAB) heard in 1886 of the proposed work and visited the church. He then sent a letter in which he put forward in the politest of terms the objections he and his committee had to the scheme. They thought the spire would be out of keeping and would add too much weight to the old tower. They considered the vestry unsuitable for two reasons: it would be difficult to heat and it would forever obliterate the remains of the old building on that site.

Mary Ann Carr daughter of the Rev. Thomas Arnold Carr, vicar 1882 to 1906. Sunday School Superintendant and the maker of the brass lectern still in use in the church.

They did not agree with removing the outside stucco, since it had evidently kept the church dry for many years, but they advocated the cutting away of the considerable growth of ivy on the south wall. Underfloor heating they thought both wasteful and harmful to floors and foundations and they objected strongly to the flue pipe from the heating system which would go up the wall near the chancel arch. They also hoped that any restoration of window tracery would indicate clearly that it was modern work and not pseudo-mediaeval.

Several letters went back and forth from the Society and the Vicarage. In the final restoration a compromise was reached. The spire was forgotten, but the vestry was built (with an extra £200 as a Queen's Jubilee gift from F.S.W. Cornwallis). The external plaster was removed, but not the ivy. Three new windows were built, two in the south aisle and one in the north. The floor was lowered four inches and the stones replaced. It is not clear who won the heating battle, for the report merely says that the church had a hot water circulation system, but the proposed flue pipe by the chancel arch did not materialise. Saving the snuffer also meant that the whole restoration cost less, which must have pleased many in the parish. The Restoration Fund raised £1,064 and the total cost was £1,062 – a very satisfactory conclusion. But with Thomas Carr organising the appeal, one could not imagine it otherwise.

In 1906 Thomas Carr retired and he and his wife and daughter went to live in Tunbridge Wells. Miss Carr gave the church the large brass lectern she had made, which is still used for festivals. The account of the farewell party leaves an impression of a respectful but affectionate congregation saying goodbye with some regret.

Chapter Six

Education in Marden

Before 1860 there was a National School run by the Church which we first hear of in Piggott's Directory in 1839. This was in a building in the churchyard and the master in 1839 was William Nettleton. There was also a school run by Mary Raban, wife of the Congregational Minister. In 1851 the Rate Book of the Overseers of the Poor records a school at Shepherd's House. In 1859 this school was called a Classical Academy with Godfrey West in charge. The National School Master in that year was George Bryant.

In 1860 the new National School was built by public subscription at a cost of about £1,600, a vast sum in those days when the average agricultural wage was twelve shillings a week. In the Long Room there is a plaque recording the opening of the building. There were three separate schools: Infants, Boys and Girls, collectively known as the National Schools. There were places for 275 children with an average attendance of 260. In 1864 a District School was built at Chainhurst with places for 60 children with an average attendance of 39. Miss Crowe was the mistress. There were other small private schools but no records survive. In 1867 Kelly's Directory tells us that James Thornhill ran a Commercial Academy and his wife Sarah a Ladies School. There is also a middle class school in connection with the Church of England held in the village with Miss Deedes (Vicar's daughter) in charge and Miss Dodson as mistress.

So there was a lively interest in education, the scholars taking their school money each week to attend school to be instructed in the three R's: Reading, Writing and Arithmetic with Needlework for the girls and Craft for the boys. A glimpse of almost any nineteenth century letter reveals the copperplate handwriting they all learned. Improving books were read, tales with a moral. The high walls and narrow windows must have echoed to the times tables, the poems, the passages from Scripture, the lists, for then education was thought to have a content to be learned. Amazingly this content often stayed with these generations who could still repeat even in their eighties and nineties what they had learned as little children. Mental Arithmetic was practised daily, as was Arithmetic addition, subtraction, multiplication, division, spelling and writing carefully in copy books. Geography and History were stories and precise lists of facts, elementary learning was something to be acquired by repetition.

The next reliable picture of education in Marden comes from the Parish Magazine for May 1884. "In February last the Government Inspection of the

81

Schools took place, and we have much pleasure in printing the Reports, which show that, in spite of the fact that the schools were closed for many weeks last year on account of illness, the results were as satisfactory as ever, and we heartily congratulate both the teachers and the children on the result of their labours . . . We are sorry to be obliged to add that there is a dark side to the picture. Owing to the amount of School-Rate not being sufficient to meet the amount of Grant earned, a deduction of £5. 10s. 10d. (£5.55) (under Article 114, New Code) has been made from the Government Grant. In other words, if £5. 10s. 10d. more had been subscribed in the Parish a sum twice this amount would have been added to the present school funds."

The last paragraph refers to the provisions of the 1870 Education Act which gave government percentage grants to existing schools and made provision for Board Schools in areas where there was not already a satisfactory voluntary school. Then follows an extract from the government report by Her Majesty's Inspector J.C. Ley, Esq., February 1884.

MARDEN PAROCHIAL SCHOOL "This School in which the attendance is never very regular, has been conducted this year under exceptional difficulties, having been closed from 20th June till 1st October owing to the prevalence of epidemic sickness. The attainments, as might have been expected, have in certain points suffered in consequence, but still, the general results are, on the whole, very satisfactory, and reflect much credit on the hard working Master and his Assistants. The children answered as hitherto readily, and for the most part well, both in Geography and Grammar, and the Recitation was fairly said. The same may be said for the Mental Arithmetic. In the Elementary subjects the first and second standards passed well, and the other standards fairly, but the work varies a good deal in quality, and Spelling is somewhat weak from the third standard upwards. Tone and order are alike very good. Needlework is creditable. A large Evening School has also been well instructed."

INFANTS SCHOOL "The Infant School (which has suffered from the same causes which have affected the Mixed School) continues in a good state of general efficiency. Some of the children write well, while others are backward in this subject."

On 19th March 1884 the Schools were inspected by the Rev. J.A. Boodle, the Diocesan Inspector. We append his reports which are most satisfactory and speak for themselves:

MARDEN PAROCHIAL SCHOOLS "The results of the Examination, though the work has been seriously interrupted during the year by epidemic sickness, were again most satisfactory. The highest group questioned by the Inspector, shewed a very good knowledge of the Scripture subjects, and in writing accurate knowledge of Prayers and Catechism. The written exercises of the second group also were creditably done, and the Catechism and other repetition

82

throughout the School were well said. The interest of the large second and third groups was remarkably well sustained by the Assistant Master and Assistant Mistress; and the answering in both classes was animated and general throughout the class."

Parchment Report. "Mr White continues to shew himself an earnest and successful Teacher; the results of the Examination are again most satisfactory."

MARDEN INFANT SCHOOL "The infants answered brightly, have learnt a good deal by heart, and sang their hymns nicely."

CHAINHURST DISTRICT SCHOOL "There was some answering in the upper group which shewed that Miss Crowe has taken the same pains as ever, with the Religious Instruction, though the children for the most part were too much inclined to allow one girl to give all the answers: in the lower group the children answered much more brightly than before. The repetition in both groups was accurately said and some of the children in the upper group wrote portions of the Catechism from memory creditably."

It would be fascinating to know what became of the girl who knew all the answers.

Mr White who featured in the report was appointed Headmaster in 1868 and served until his death in 1908. Mr White's family was also involved with the school. In May 1884 the Parish Magazine records that his son Robert T. White was the church organist and that his daughter Edna was awarded the needlework prize for standard 4. Mr White's elder daughter Priscilla taught in the school from January 1895 until her marriage on 2nd August 1896. The School Log Book records that "the Headmaster was absent from school on that day from 1.45pm till 3pm to attend the marriage ceremony of his eldest daughter, the school being left in charge of Mr Kemsley and the monitors". A nice devotion to duty to be absent for only an hour and a quarter. Edna White was appointed assistant teacher in October 1897 and resigned to be married nine years later in 1906. In 1900 Robert T. White, by then Dr White Mus. Doc. Oxon as his father records in the Log Book, examined the First Class in "that singing by note that has been taught them throughout the year". Later in 1900 Robert was left in charge of the school when his father visited Canterbury. So the White family living in the school house for forty years must have almost become a village institution. Indeed village tradition tells us that Mr White was known affectionately to all his scholars as 'Daddy White'.

The official School Log Book dates from 1st April 1895 when A. Horrell, Clerk, wrote "I am directed by the School Board to inform you that the terms of the transfer of the National Schools have been temporarily accepted. The Board have decided to retain the services of the whole of the present staff of Teachers at their present salaries subject to revision at a further meeting. I am also directed to call upon you and the other teachers to cease teaching the Church Catechism in the Schools." Thus Marden Schools ceased to be denominational.

There was an area of disagreement concerning the take over and on 7th August 1895 Mr White was informed by Mr Fowles, Clerk, that the Board was unable to come to terms with the Committee in the matter of the transfer of the School Buildings. "I am instructed to give you one month's notice in accordance with the resolution passed on 1st April the terms of which said resolution you accepted by letter dated April 3rd." The Board resolved that the School should be closed from 19th August. Reason must have prevailed for on 24th September Mr Fowles informed Mr White that "the Board having come to terms with the School Committee have decided to re-open the Schools on Monday next the 30th instant".

Mr White duly reopened the Schools after six weeks holiday, 184 present and the usual staff except Mr Jones "who is waiting the Board's decision re - increase of salary before returning". Times do not change.

In July 1897 the girls were separated from the boys and Miss Lloyd was appointed Headmistress. Miss Lloyd notes in her Log Book that on 10th August 1897 Reverend T.A. Carr and Miss Carr visited. On the 17th August Mr F.D. Bray visited and checked the registers. In 1898 the elections to the School Board were as follows:

Elected	E. Day New Member	347 votes
	G. Manwaring	330 votes
	J. Carpenter	267 votes
	Rev. T.A. Carr	266 votes
	Dr Smart New Member	260 votes
Not Elected	F. Bray Old Member	228 votes
	W. Tassell	219 votes
	H. Crowhurst Old Member	207 votes

Three years later fortunes had changed

Elected	F. Bray	445 votes
	H. Crowhurst	317 votes
	Rev. T.A. Carr	300 votes
	G. Manwaring	297 votes
	E. Day	295 votes
Not Elected	J. Carpenter	249 votes
	Dr Smart	206 votes
	F.W. Tippen	108 votes

These local residents elected to the Board worked hard on behalf of the Schools and were well known to parents and children.

On 3rd May 1898 Mr White records that "Rev. T.A. Carr again visited and incidentally questioned the First Class on some geographical points in reference to the present war between the United States and Spain. He expressed much gratification at their general knowledge of the same." The heat wave of 1900 was recorded; in July there were several cases of fainting in school owing to the excessive heat, temperature 80° to 88° F. In April of that year the Headmaster wrote "cautioned the whole school against interfering in any way with the pipes that are now being laid through the village in connection with the new water

Boys' school group. Robert White, Headmaster at right.

supply". On 7th May from 3.30pm to 4pm Mr White took the First Class boys into the playground and gave them a lesson on the partial eclipse of the sun which was then taking place and distinctly visible with the naked eye but more so when observed through smoked pieces of glass.

On 30th November a London photographer took portraits at noon in three groups in the boys' playground. 131 scholars present. School photographs were taken again in 1904 and 1906. Could the illustrations be these? On 6th May 1901 permission was given by the Board for boys to play on the new recreation ground and Mr White formed cricket clubs for older and younger boys and necessary materials were purchased for the same. Practices were allowed 12 noon to 1.30pm each day and in the evening after 4pm under certain conditions. Mr White did not say what these were.

On the 21st April 1902 Miss Lloyd notes that three new shelves have been placed in the dinner lodge for the baskets of the distant children who bring their dinners. 1st May Mr White comments that "Scarcely any children absent today exhibiting May Garlands, (round the village) which has been a distinguishing feature in this Parish for 40 years past on May Day". Old customs were already dying out. "16th May taught to the whole school (by request of the Board) a new verse to the National Anthem appropriate to the recent Peace declaration (end of the Boer War) and the forthcoming Coronation festivities. 20th May closed the School at 4pm for next week's Coronation holidays."

20th June Miss Lloyd records that "four girls from Dr Banardo's have left school this week as they are leaving for Canada shortly". Two years later 18th June "Adrian Hagemeyer, Harry May and Albert Mannock (orphans from the Gordon Boys Homes) left this school to return there, owing to their foster parents in this village losing the supervision of them by Miss Carr our late vicar's daughter." "19th August 1906 Annie and Lily Brill left the Girls School to return to Dr Banardo's Home previous to their departure for Canada." So there is evidence for a tradition of fostering in the village.

Miss Lloyd liked to note the school songs the girls learned. "Give me a draught" did this meet with general approval? "Before all lands" yes certainly. "Through lanes with hedgerows pearly" "The Seasons" and "Winter time brings joy and mirth" no doubt inspired the year of 1898. The following year the girls were singing "A Spring Song", "Wild Wood Flowers", "Never forget the dear ones", "Home" and "Up in the morning's cheerful light". I hope they learned that in the summer.

Agriculture was the main occupation of the village in the nineteenth and early twentieth centuries and the Schools followed the agricultural year. If children passed the examination for Labour Certificates held at Yalding they were allowed to attend school as Half-Timers. 3rd March 1902 14 boys took the exam.

Age last birthday	Name	Attendances
11	Ernest Price	321
12	Percy Waghorne	128
12	Charles Gilbert	342
12	George Burr	327
13	Henry Gaskin	351
13	Leslie Jarrett	354
13	William Bateup	345
12	Jas Edmund	278
12	Reg Gainsford	240
13	John Bufford	178
12	George Norris	133
12	Jack Judge	191
13	Albert Crowhurst	233
12	Albert Robbins	349
13	Sydney Ellis	282

By 10th March the Headmaster was noting that there were "Frequent enquiries by the parents of those children who gained their Labour Certificates at the Yalding Exam as to the earliest date their boys may leave for the Summer's agricultural work".

Girls also took the exam in 1902 and Miss Lloyd notes that Lily Lindridge and Nellie Taylor, having passed standard 5, are now eligible for total exemption. Edith Onions, Elsie Osborne, Winnie Vidler, Flossie Skinner and Lily Waterman have qualified as half timers. On 12th October 1903 Mr White wrote in the Log

A girls' school group. Behind: the former National School before conversion to the Memorial Hall.

Book "More half-timers (who have mostly been absent all the summer months at field work) returned to school for the winter months. Find recapitulation of work necessary that was taught before they left. Some of the usual Michaelmas migration taking place amongst the agricultural labourers and their children. A few boys admitted from a private venture school in the village." Another small private school must have closed for some reason.

In May 1895 we hear that the average attendances (of upper standards chiefly) are decreasing owing to hop tying, but not to the same extent as in former years. Miss Lloyd has the same difficulties and writes 12th May 1899 "Attendance not good children assisting their parents in hop tying". Miss Lloyd again notes absences on 12th July for Currant Picking. The same problem in April 1902 "Applications from parents respecting permission for their children to temporarily absent themselves from school to assist them in hop tying". The Headmaster requests all such applicants to make personal interviews to the Board at their monthly meeting as on former occasions.

26th August 1902 "the ordinary drawing lesson from 3pm to 4pm suspended today for the Headmaster to give a special lesson to the 1st Class on Hop Picking Accounts particularly Tallying sums which are found to be of a practical nature and useful during the picking season".

On the 29th August Mr White closed the School for the Hop Picking Holiday until 5th October. However on 26th September he writes "Owing to the Hop Picking of the larger farmers lasting longer than was anticipated and thus causing several children to be employed next week the Board have decided to extend the holidays for another week. Parents notified accordingly".

8th February 1907 The Inspector wrote in the Government Report "standards 1 and 2 made very fair progress in their work, but the other standards are backwards and shew poor results under examination. The boys seem willing enough but they do not appear to have been sufficiently trained in habits of industry and attention. Seven of the boys in the 1st Class who were present on the day of my visit had been absent during the summer months of last year". Above this Mr White had written "Query fourteen?" helping to explain further the difficulties of bringing the class up to what the Inspector considered to be the required standard.

As the Inspector's report for 1884 confirmed the Schools were often closed for epidemic illness. The dreaded diseases for children were diphtheria, scarlet fever, whooping cough and measles. On 2nd December 1898 there were a number of children with scarlet fever and on 13th December Miss Lloyd fell victim to the disease herself. She resumed her duties on 22nd January 1899. In February children were absent from school because the roads were flooded after recent heavy rains. Miss Lloyd "punished several first class girls for quitting the playground without permission during recess to see the flood in the adjoining fields". There are still floods after heavy rain but the Local Drainage Board has improved the situation in the Low Weald. On 10th February there was still scarlet fever about and on the 24th a fresh case was reported in the family of Vowsden at Cheveney.

The following March 1899 Miss Lloyd was again,ill this time with pneumonia and congestion of the lungs. But there was news to cheer her when she returned to school "My Lords have sanctioned the omission of the annual inspection of the Girls' School due in February 1900".

12th November 1901 Mr White writes "owing to the continued spread of diphtheria in the Parish and the deaths of two children recently attending the Schools Dr Tew, Medical Officer of Health, in conjunction with the School Board officially ordered the closing of all the departments from this date till the thirtieth instant".

On 1st December "another case of diphtheria having occurred a further closure has been ordered by Dr Tew till after the Christmas holidays. All the school rooms have been disinfected".

11th January 1905 "As the epidemic of measles continues to increase (over 100 cases being reported) Dr Tew has ordered further closure of the Schools until the 27th instant".

11th January 1905 "As the epidemic of Measles has not sufficiently abated another week's closure has officially been ordered. The Schools to be re-opened Monday February 5th".

In the summer of 1906 on 22nd June the Headmaster reported "a few cases of absentees through whooping cough this week. Care was taken to exclude from school any children in a family suffering from the complaint by Doctor's orders".

On 26th June there was tempestuous weather "a large acacia tree in front of the Headmaster's house was blown down by the fierce wind this morning". The following week on 6th July "whooping cough continues to spread amongst children in the Parish".

15th October Fred Packham, standard 4 was sent by the Headmaster to Dr Ainsworth to be examined for suspected ringworm. The boy was ordered to stay away from school till 15th November and a Doctor's Certificate obtained and filed according to Kent Education Committee's instructions. 16th November "An outbreak of Measles reported amongst two families in the Parish. Caution given to parents by the attendance officer against sending any child to school from an infected family".

22nd December "As the epidemic of Measles is still raging a special meeting of the Managers by the local Doctor's advice resolved to extend the School holidays for another week. The School to be re-opened on 7th January 1907".

When the Schools were visited on 21st January by C.W. Hitchens he noted "the rooms are cold today the thermometer below 50 F" not exactly conducive to academic concentration".

7th June Mr Crowhurst, manager, called to enquire if there were any very poor children in the school who appeared to be underfed thus being unable to attend to their studies properly. K.E.C. had required such cases to be investigated. The Headmaster did not know of any during the summer, but in the winter when parents were sometimes out of work occasional cases occurred of apparent destitution both of food and clothing. The Relieving Officer, however, generally attended to any serious conditions.

6th January 1908 "Measles have broken out in the family of Manktelow, Railway Cottages, and all scholars ordered to remain at home during the usual quarantine period, as per code".

A sad entry in the Girls School Log 9th June 1913 "Sareh Godden sent home from school. 13th June Sareh Godden died in the fever hospital. Parents seem afraid to send their children to school". The School was closed till 24th June and then till 14th July. Meanwhile the Teachers washed out the cupboards with Sanitas and burned all manuscript paper and old books. All the needlework of the girls with fever was destroyed. 8th March 1907 Miss Tidd was ordered a month's rest as she was suffering from anaemia and Mr White applied to K.E.C. for a temporary substitute.

13th April Mr James Crouch, an unattached teacher was sent to Marden.

25th May Mr Crouch suddenly expired from pneumonia and on the 27th Mr White was absent from school from 2.30pm to 3.30pm to attend Mr Crouch's funeral service at Marden Church.

Thus without the benefits of modern medical discoveries children, parents and teachers struggled with disease at the beginning of the century. On 17th January 1906 the Headmaster had given a lesson on Parliamentary General Elections to the 1st Class instead of the usual Geography lesson. The following day the school was closed for polling Ashford Division Hardy v. Harris. The results of this election brought into office the Liberal Government which in March 1906 passed a School Meals Act that permitted local education authorities to provide free meals for school children if they felt a need existed and in 1907 an Act requiring schools to carry out Medical Inspections. In 1908 this same government introduced a non contributory Old Age Pension of 5 shillings (25p) a week for single people over the age of seventy and 7s. 6d. (35p) for married couples. These measures improved conditions and Miss Lloyd notes that in March 1909 19 girls were presented for Medical Inspection and the following March 27 girls were medically examined. On 5th May 1911 Miss Lloyd received a Medical Log Book from K.E.C.

School was not all Inspectors' Reports, epidemics and getting time off for agricultural work. There were the holidays and children's treats. On 24th June 1895 the Board directed Mr Fowles to inform Mr White that he was "authorised to close the Schools on the afternoon of such days on which children's treats are given until further notice". Two days later "A holiday given this afternoon (according to foregoing resolution) on the occasion of the Providence Chapel annual Sunday School Treat held at Mr Crowhurst's Farm. 3rd July a similar holiday given for the annual Day School Treat conducted by Mr F.D. Bray and held in Mr Mayris' field. About 500 children were present". Where did they all come from? "10th July The Annual Foresters Fete was held in the village and the customary whole holiday given. 17th July The Church Sunday School Annual Treat held in the Vicarage grounds. 24th July Annual Excursion of the Church Choir and several parishioners to Hastings and the usual whole holiday given. 31st July the Annual Wesleyan Sunday School Treat held in the afternoon and a holiday given as per resolution."

In October 1900 the power to grant holidays by Head Teachers was rescinded, but the annual treats and holidays continued. On 15th April 1902 a holiday was given to attend Julian's travelling circus which was in the village. After the summer holidays of 1906 Miss Lloyd noted that "the School had been redecorated, desks varnished and repaired, ceilings white washed, walls coloured and the playground retarred and sanded".

6th July 1906 "The Annual Day School Treat eastablished twenty-two years ago for all the children living in the Parish and attending these or neighbouring schools held in Mr Reader's field".

25th July "Customary whole holiday for the Annual Church Choir and Parish excursion to Ramsgate and Margate".

On 3rd August the Annual Church Sunday School Treat was held in the Vicarage field and a whole holiday was given by order of the Committee.

The following year for the Annual Sunday School Treat the older children and teachers were taken to the Crystal Palace superintended by the vicar. On 28th June 1909 School closed early to permit the children to attend the dedication service of the Tower and Bells taken by the Bishop of Croydon. 30th June was noted as the second day of Marden Bazaar and very many boys were absent. Comment on 2nd July was that the various attractions in the village had greatly interfered with school attendance. Finally on 3rd July a Cricket Match, School v. Marden Choir. Scores School 183, S. Hayes 118 and the Choir 19 and 55. Did S. Hayes go on to a cricketing career?

A much sterner view was taken of winter absentees from school. 6th November "A few boys absent today preparing for the annual village Bonfire Demonstration this evening. The attendance Officer informed of the same." Should the date have been the 5th? Worse was to follow on 22nd November "Some boys illegally absent this week assisting shooters of game in the Parish. Names were sent to the Attendance Officer who promised to lay the matter before the Maidstone School Attendance Committee with a view to prosecution of both Employers and Parents".

The children of Marden and District competed for scholarships from the Sir Charles Booth Charity of £10 per year for two to five years. This must have seemed a large sum of money in 1898 when Gertrude Judd and Joseph Pettet were successful. On 29th March 1900 Charles Lefeaver and Fred Manktelow gained Charles Booth scholarships and it was noted that their aggregate marks were higher than the three girls who also competed. On 7th May Charles Lefeaver aged thirteen and Fred Manktelow twelve left to attend the Tonbridge Commercial School as day scholars. On 26th March 1902 Albert Crowhurst aged thirteen was awarded a scholarship. On 17th April the Headmaster of Tonbridge Commercial School sent this post card "Dear Mr White, Much obliged by the receipt of Crowhurst's character. You have sent us some good working boys whom it is a pleasure to teach. With all kind wishes, Your very truly, W.J.D. Bryant". Praise for Mr White and for Marden. The next year on 6th April 1903 William Reader was awarded a Booth Scholarship. Mr White writes "he intends continuing his education at Rev. Kendon's Secondary School Goudhurst (Bethany) or at Tonbridge".

So from the village school at the turn of the century there was a steady if small number of children continuing their education at specialised schools. Perhaps this helped to counteract the feeling of the Inspector's Report for March 1900 "I shall look for better work and more intelligence at future visits" and again in 1901 "intelligence is not generally conspicuous in this school". Perhaps the Inspector had just had a bad day.

Chapter Seven

The Parish Council

The Local Government Act of 1894 meant the end of the old Vestry, for this Act set up Parish Councils for the first time. After the New Poor Law Amendment Act of 1834, however, the Vestry had already begun to lose some of its total responsibility for the well-being and support of its own villagers. Now the Parish Council took over the running of village affairs (under the ultimate control of the new Rural District Council) and the traditional intertwining of church and laity in organising village life was gone for ever. The laws of the land were brought down from Parliament through the Maidstone Rural District Council to Marden, instead of through the magistrates to the Vestry, as they had been since Queen Elizabeth I's days.

There were twenty-six candidates for eleven places on the first Parish Council elected on 4th December 1894. The members chosen were:

Frank Bray	Albert Pettett
Joseph Carpenter	Alfred Reeves
Edward Day	Stephen Stanley
Ernest Honess	Walter Taylor
James Mercer Jnr.	Frederick Tippen
	Spencer Thomas

One of the early improvements made in the village was the provision of gas lighting, first suggested in 1900 by Frederick Tippen. In 1904 the Mid Kent Gas Light and Coke Company agreed to light, extinguish and repair lamps for £2. 3s. 9d. each (£2.19) per annum. They were lit with varying degrees of efficiency until 1915 when their use was forbidden during the First World War. The company had in fact been about to terminate its agreement with the parish because of rising costs, so it was not surprising that the Council did not make a fresh agreement until 1923.

Water and sewage were ever problems in a rural area and Marden had its share of these. Late in 1907 the Town Pump, the village water supply was locked up by the Rural District Council when they found " . . . considerable quantities of organic matter, ammonia, nitrates and chlorides in the drinking water". Many farms however relied on their own wells for many more years, though this was not always a wise course; there was typhoid at Hertsfield Farm in the 1920s.

Thomas Fowle. Born 1846. High Street grocer, Assistant Overseer to the Poor and Collector of Taxes. At the formation of the first Parish Council in 1894 he became Clerk to the Parish Council. Photographed in his eighties.

In 1915, too, the Local Government Board's inspector found that the existing sewage system, which otherwise worked quite well, emptied into an open ditch which ran along the back of the schools and it needed immediate attention. The Medical Officer of Health said that " . . . the problem is a great nuisance", but he would not say it was the cause of increased infection. In fact there had been a fair amount of time lost at school through sickness of the children. The sewage problem was not satisfactorily solved until the new sewage works opened in 1933.

Another problem that had teased the village for some time was that of a full churchyard. Despite the nineteenth century extension, the need for extra land became urgent in the 1920s and in 1930 the Parish Council bought ground from Thomas Judd for a cemetery. A suggestion that a chapel be built at the same time was voted out.

During the first thirty-nine years of the life of the Parish Council, Thomas Fowle was Clerk. The minutes he wrote, clear, painstakingly annotated and elegant are a legacy of his fifty years of service to the village as Clerk, Assistant Overseer, Clerk to the School Board, member of the Vestry and Church warden – in addition to running a grocer's shop.

In February 1889, at a time when farming had begun its decline, a public meeting was held at the National Schools, under the chairmanship of J. Hartridge, to " . . . consider the possibility of forming an Agricultural Association for Marden and District". The Rev. Thomas Carr joined the meeting and voted with the others present for such an association to be formed. In this way the very popular ploughing match competitions became an annual event, organised by the association, whose official title was 'The Marden, Staplehurst and Collier Street Agricultural Association'.

Richard Hollamby, waggoner for many years to Mrs Harriet Hammond, Cornwells Farm, with team and mate. In spite of a wooden leg he won many prizes at the Ploughing Match including Long Service awards in 1889 and 1906.

The aim of the members was specifically to encourage those who worked on farms, at a time when farming prospects were a trifle gloomy. When W.H. and H. Le May, hop factors, offered a prize to the grower of the best growth of hops, the committee turned the offer down, noting that the Association was formed with the object of " . . . encouragement for the labourers, more than the employers".

There were normally classes for wheel ploughs, foot ploughs and later on iron ploughs, which, despite a doubling of the prize money, never became popular. Hop dryers could enter samples of hops and shepherds with flocks of over a hundred ewes, or less than a hundred could also compete. Awards were given for 'meritorious service' of farm workers and women who worked in the house. The best turned out teams of horses also gained prizes.

One of the most regular contestants was Richard Hollamby who, despite a wooden leg, took many prizes for ploughing. He worked for Henry Hammond at Cornwell's.

The Association kept its eye on all things connected with farming, from complaining to the South Eastern and Chatham Railway in 1910 that farm produce was not being loaded or shunted carefully enough (and receiving a detailed and courteous reply) to asking the General Post Office why it was not supplying telephones in Marden as it had done in Linton. The reply to the last question was that not enough people in Marden and Staplehurst had given the scheme their support and guarantees would be necessary from each parish before the telephones would be installed.

At the outbreak of the 1914 war, the Association was wound up and the accumulated money was handed over to the fund for the relief of Belgian refugees, a popular charity of the time.

Prize List for 1908

Class One: Champion Wheel Ploughs   Employer
1. W. Watts   H. Watts   A. and P. Honess
2. A. Farmer   C. Farmer   W. Tipples
3. J. Dicker   J. Dicker Jnr.   T. and G. Oyler
4. G. Morphey   W. Underdown   W. Tompsett Jnr.

Class Two: Wheel Ploughs
1. J. Skinner   H. Skinner   W. Tassell
2. G. Smith   R. Smith   F.S.W. Cornwallis
3. J. Ford   C. Judge   R. Hartridge
4. T. Peckham   T. Butler   Manwaring and Tassell

Class Three: Foot Ploughs
1. F. Stone   J. Mankelow   T. and G. Oyler
2. J. Meades   L. Wallis   C.M. Fox
3. T. Farmer   E. Farmer   D.A. Seligman
4. F. Fuggle   G. Fuggle   G. Jenner

Class Four: Horse Ploughs | Employer
1. W. Peckham | T.S.D. Spencer
2. A. Coomber | F. Manwaring
3. J. Golding | H. and T. Manwaring
4. R. Hollamby | H. Hammond

Laurence Hardy Prize for Best Turned Out Teams
1. G. Morris   W. Williams   W. Highwood
2. J. Wratten   G. Guilliam   F. Manwaring
3. J. Meades   L. Wallis   C.M. Fox

Special Prize for Best Turned Out Team for Pair Horses (first year)
1. A. Coomber | F. Manwaring
2. W. Peckham | T.P.D. Spencer

Hop Drying Competition (52 entries)
1. C. Judge | C. Hanmer
2. R. Hadaway | T. and G. Oyler
3. John Mankelow | D.A. Seligman
4. Frank King | T. and G. Oyler

Shepherds. Over 100 Ewes
1. H. Parsons | C.M. Fox
2. F. Thompson | R. Hartridge
3. D. Haffenden | T. Wipples

Shepherds. Under 100 Ewes
1. J. Harman | J. Weeks
2. A. Bailey | M.J. Bourner
3. J. Meades | Britcher and Sons

Meritorious Service
1. Geo. Smith   16 years   F.S.W. Cornwallis
2. W. Bugden   16 years   T. and G. Oyler
3. A. Rhodes   16 years   William Tassell
4. J.Meafer   15 years 9 months   F.S.W. Cornwallis
5. S. Golding   15 years 1 month   A. and P. Honess
6. V. Russell   14years 1 month   C.M. Fox

Female Domestic Servants
1. Nancy Brown   5 years 1 month   A. Crowhurst
2. Daisy H. Young 47 years 6 months   R. Cole
3. Rose Gorham   47 years 3 months   F. Manwaring

Chapter Eight

Into the Twentieth Century

1900-1939

At the Parish Council meeting on 11th June 1907, Councillors Le Feaver and White proposed that the Clerk ask the County Council to erect three 'Motor Danger' signs at Stile Bridge, Bumpers' Hall and the Beech Cross roads; the use of cars was increasing in the village. On the same occasion, Councillor Le Feaver said he was concerned about the difficulty of finding enough room at the Stile Bridge road juntion safely to turn a waggon and team of horses – the forge took up a lot of the available space.

These two items appear to sum up the change in the countryside which occurred between the turn of the century and the start of the Second World War, particularly during the 1920s and '30s. The old and the new were juxtaposed: the farm orientated life of the village continued but modern ideas, new inventions and the cold economic climate of post 1918 changed many of the practices and the lives of those who lived in Marden. For one thing, the large Cornwallis estate, which in Marden had totalled 2,347 acres at its peak, was sold up and the tenants encouraged to buy their properties.

The decline in farming, evident in Marden from the late 1880s when the arable acreage tumbled, was arrested by the First World War. Food imports could not now be relied upon and farmers were encouraged to grow corn. In fact in Marden the corn did not increase much (687 acres in 1901 to 698 acres in 1917), but cattle, sheep and pig populations grew and more orchards were planted, carrying on the pre-war trend: 788 acres in 1901, 1,402 acres in 1914 and 1,576 acres by 1917. Fruit, like hops, bore a controlled price and was well worth growing. In 1918 forty pound cases of fruit sold for 20s. 10d. (£1.05) – almost half a farm worker's wages for a week.

In 1917, too, the Board of Agriculture appointed a Hop-Controller, George Foster Clark of Maidstone, to set the price of hops. Hop acreage was to be cut to half the 1914 level, a strange decision which must have been regretted by the armed services and was certainly not repeated for the Second World War. The growers, however, appreciated the price which Foster Clark fixed for 1918: £16. 10s. (£16.50) per hundredweight; it must have sweetened the job of grubbing good hop gardens. Nothing approaching that price had been paid since the disastrous harvest of 1882. It is no wonder that the newly formed National

Robert Oyler (right), Pattenden Farm, in an early motor car.

Robert Oyler, Pattenden, in his Sunbeam car, said once to have belonged to Sir Henry Seagrave.

House at Marden Beech known as 'Old Sally's', long since demolished. In front the Butler family from Cornwells. About 1910.

Farmers' Union were hoping that control for hops would continue in the depressed years that followed the end of the war.

As farm prices sank, however, after 1918, farm wages fell with them. In December 1921 Captain James Scott said at a local NFU meeting " . . . Can any worker with a young family, at the present cost of living, exist on less than 36 shillings a week?" Wages had been 39 shillings in 1917. Nonetheless, the branch of the NFU recorded a wage of 27 shillings (£1.35) in 1923, with 7d. (3p) an hour for overtime. Wheat prices fell from 75s. 6d. (£3.78) in 1919 to 40s. 0d. (£2) in 1921. Confidence in a future for the traditional mixed farming of the Weald disintegrated; the NFU journals of the time were full of advice on poultry farming and the care of milking herds, as arable land lapsed into grass. However, the fruit trade continued to expand and Marden growers had plenty of expert advice from the enlarged East Malling Research Station.

In December 1927 the Marden branch of the NFU passed a resolution: "That this meeting is of the opinion that Home Grown Fruit should be more extensively advertised and that a better system of distribution should be organised". To these ends, and in order to raise the standards of growing and packing fruit, local growers formed the 'Marden and District Fruit Show Society' which held its first

Hop pickers at Chainhurst Farm in 1916.

Hop pickers at Chainhurst Farm in 1916. The cookhouse.

100

Hop-picking at Chainhurst Farm in 1916. Left to right: — Packham, measurer; William Ashdown, dryer; Wm Ashdown, jr; Horace Butler, farmer.

show in 1933. This became and still is an important part of the farming year. In 1935, however, it was cancelled after a May frost of twelve degrees Fahrenheit and severe gales in the following September. Many growers in that year did not pick a single apple. By that time there were 2,160 acres of fruit in Marden.

Despite these problems, however, life and work went on in the village. Farm men had always been versatile: the variety of jobs they did in any two weeks of the year ensured this. Now in addition to the expertise they had in handling and judging crops, animals and simple building, they became increasingly involved in engineering as tractors, lorries and harvesting machinery became more common. There was a Saunderson tractor at Pattenden farm in the early 1900s and a little later there were Titans in the village. After Henry Ford's entry into the market, Fordsons became very popular.

One of the traditional tasks which changed was that of droving. Most men who did this job have a tale which only retrospectively seemed funny. Jim Butler tells of the day when three fat cattle ran off in the Tonbridge Road, Maidstone, on their way down to the market. They lumbered into the grounds of Edward Sharp's house (the sweet manufacturer) and created havoc on the tennis court which was just being made. When the harassed Jim Butler finally reached the market, he was chided by the RSPCA inspector for chasing animals.

Hop pickers at Chainhurst Farm in 1916.

Chainhurst Farm oast. Hop-picking 1916.

102

Cornwells Farm. Packing apples for the first Marden Fruit Show in 1933.

Harry Burr, too, received sharp words from a housewife in Loose, when one of the cows he was taking to be sold galloped into a back garden and stuck its head round the kitchen door. Going to Horsmonden Lamb Fair was difficult, too. With thousands of sheep arriving, shepherds had to make sure the flocks did not become mixed in what looked like a carpet of wool on the roads leading into Horsmonden.

Gradually, however, people realised just how much weight and condition animals lost on these journeys and farmers began to use motor transport. In 1928 Frank Botten and Charlie Luck started a business as coal merchants and hauliers. They soon built up the haulage side of their enterprise, taking animals to and from markets and delivering fertilisers. They also delivered coal seven days a week and on Bank Holidays if need be — 2s. 2d. a hundredweight in summer and 2s. 4d. in winter (11p and 12p). Charlie Luck, a cheerful, popular figure, carried on the business after his partner died and his lorry travelled round the routes to and from the market as he completed fifty years of trading.

The railway, even earlier, had taken over from man and waggon (note the fruit carriage from the C.M. Fox farms in 1887). In the first part of the twentieth century the train was an important trade link. Young Bessie Osborne of Dairy

FORDSON

You Will Want Your Fordson Tractor Early

Everything points to the greatest shortage of Ford products this year that has ever existed.

Never before has the demand been so great.

You will want a Fordson Tractor early—here is one product you cannot wait for—when the weather opens up you will need it.

You will want it for ploughing, seeding, cultivating—and all your other work. Already it has proved the greatest help to profitable farming that has ever been offered you. And at £120 at Works, Manchester, the price is so low that you lose money every day you are without a Fordson.

To get delivery you must order early.

ORDER NOW from the Authorised Dealers:

HAYNES BROS, Ltd.,
FORD DEPOT,
King Street, MAIDSTONE.

£120

At Works,
Manchester.

An early farm tractor. The Fordson was to become the standard workhorse of the area until well after the second world war.

104

Cornwells Farm. An early Fordson tractor, driver Percy Rapson, drawing a mower with Richard Hollamby on the seat.

Farm, growing up in the years before 1914, liked to watch the shunting, loading and unloading which went on every day at Marden station. This continued until the Second World War; road transport relieved some of the congestion of traffic at the station, but did not pose a threat to rail freight until after 1945. Indeed, in 1922 the NFU was so concerned at the long wait farm produce had before it was loaded into the trains that it tried unsuccessfully to persuade the Southern Railway to make a siding at Collier Street.

By the time Alfred Winter came to Marden station as porter signalman in 1924, the yard was often so full of bulky items like shoddy, feathers, coal, fruit baskets and other items that a man was employed especially to sweep and tidy up. During the 1930s a train known as 'The Bullet' was put on to deal with the fruit traffic; the wagons were fitted out and had brakes so that the loads could travel with the minimum of movement to avoid bruising. The train started from Headcorn, but however full the train was by the time it reached Marden, the parish produced a still bigger amount for the journey to London.

Hop picking created many problems (but a great deal of revenue) for the railway. In addition to the several thousand pickers which the Southern Railway transported from London to Marden, it had to cope with the many visitors who arrived to visit relations and friends over the weekend.

The village itself was transformed during the weeks of September. All these immigrants had to eat and hop picking was an important addition to the local traders' takings, both in public houses and the shops. As hop picking started

The NEW
SAUNDERSON
Super Light-Weight
TRACTOR

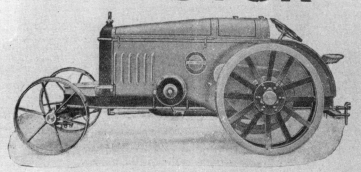

Capable of pulling 3 Furrows
in average 3 Horse Land and
2 FURROWS in ANY Land.

Power: 20 B.H.P., weight
28 cwt. ; fitted with
ROLLER BEARINGS
Lubricating oil economy
approximate 1 pint oil
per day throughout
whole Tractor.

£195

3 YEARS' GUARANTEE
The Highest Grade Tractor in the World.

Write for Catalogue and Particulars.

The SAUNDERSON TRACTOR & IMPLEMENT Cº LTD
ELSTOW WORKS, BEDFORD.

Telephone : Bedford 788.

An early farm tractor. There was a Saunderson working at Pattenden in the early 1920s.

The staff at Marden Station

tradesmen erected temporary wire netting windows or fittings on their counters, since the invasion of so many Londoners appeared slightly threatening as well as profitable. Even opening hours were geared to the hop pickers' needs. Ken Ballard, whose father owned one of the butchers' shops, said, "If we heard that one of the farms was going to be late getting its hops picked that day, we'd stay open until they'd finished, so they could get their meat". On Saturdays he and his sister used to sell vegetables and apples outside their father's shop — pot herbs to go with the stewing meat. They often sold a ton of potatoes during the day. Other stalls in the village sold cold fried fish, peanuts, jellied eels and cheese cakes.

The Hop Pickers' Mission (where the Medical Centre is now) took care of any ailments and minor accidents among the pickers. The Mission, given by Mrs Spender of Chantry Place, also looked after sick orphans during the rest of the year.

The pickers usually went to the same farms every year; children were born and grew up knowing the same yearly holiday. Some had grandmothers who had

107

Marden Station at the beginning of the nineteenth century.

Local ice cream van in the hop garden. Whittles had a shop below the Chequers and took ice cream around in this Austin 7 car.

Hop picking. The poke cart. Hertsfield Farm waggoner William Payne on the cart. These hops are grown on wirework and the wires can be seen remaining after the hops are picked.

made the journey for decades. It was a matriarchal affair, bins were handed down from mother to daughter and letters booking for the following season arrived as soon as Christmas was over. For many people the word 'September' did not exist: events of the year were dated 'before hop picking' or 'after hop picking'.

After it was all over, the long good humoured queue formed for the final Pay Off and then they went back to London, the children's winter shoes assured and a little bit of money besides. The village took down its wire netting, packed away the bins and measurers' baskets and settled down to winter.

The Saw Mill

Another busy part of Marden was Harry Bridgland's saw mill at the West End. A great deal of wood was used in pre-1939 days, when the plastics industry was in its infancy, quite enough for a village to support its own small wood industry.

Frank Wood, who worked at the mill, says that Harry Bridgland had a masterly eye for estimating the volume of wood in a standing tree, a necessary skill from the business point of view.

"Once we were in Mote Park and we decided to have a bet on how much a certain tree would produce. We spent ages working it out (we weren't very old), when Harry came along and said 'What are you boys up to?' When we told him

Marden Methodist Sunday School Party. C.1896.

Wade's Butcher's shop. Now Turnpike House. Harry Wade, right, in cart. Eric Hayes with cycle.

Portable shop which once stood in front of the West End forge.

he asked if he could join in. Then he glanced at the tree and put his bet in. When we had measured it after felling, he went off with our money in his pocket."

After the trees were cut down, they were hauled up on to a timber tug with the aid of a traction engine. The mill supplied felloes for wheelwrights, all kinds of timber for builders, plough and harrow beams, cart rods, thousands of riven fence poles for the Linton Park estate and even crucks for Rye fishing boats.

Church Going

In the 1920s and '30s there was opportunity, if not always enthusiasm, for visiting a variety of churches and chapels in the parish. So much so that a writer in the 'Kent Messenger' in 1933 said: "Marden is no worse than any other village as regards church going, but it must hold a record for the number of churches and chapels in proportion to its population". The parish church had in addition two missions, at Chainhurst and at the Mile Bush. In 1895 Henry Crowhurst had given the village what became known as the 'Providence Chapel'; the Methodist church, housed in a handsome building, stood where its remains, the Vestry Hall, stand today.

West End Forge. Tyring a wheel. Left W. Lavender, wheelwright and right G.A. Rootes, blacksmith.

West End Forge. Shoeing. The waggoner holds the horse, the apprentice rasps the hoof.

At the Beech Chapel there was another group of Methodists, while at Chainhurst C.M. Fox of Dairy Farm had built the Gospel Hall for the use of the village. The Congregational Church continued to thrive, as it still does today. For those who liked something different on Sunday evenings, particularly in summer, there was the service at Blantyre House, Goudhurst, Mr Fegan's home for orphaned boys, where worshippers from the surrounding parishes were always welcome.

It was the Congregational minister, the Rev. S.J. Kingsbury, who said in 1933, "What we want in the country parishes is a united Free Church. I have thought about it for a long time, but it is difficult to get people to move in the matter".

Fifty years later there is perhaps more feeling of church unity than there was in the '30s, when for a population of about 2,500 people there were eight places of worship.

A Village Changing

Until 1939 Marden was still able to supply most of the needs of the parish. Groceries, meat, milk, fruit, vegetables, baked goods, clothes, haircuts, tools, ironmongery, bicycles, cars, alcohol, even funerals could all be found within the village. J.H. Sutton and Sons, Crowhurst and Tompsett and George Twyman and Son all supplied farm needs. S.F. Stanley and Sons built houses, arranged funerals and could supply a touring car in 1924 for £110. R. Miskin and Son sold coal, coke, hay and straw.

Albion Road looking into the High Street. This end of Albion Road was once called 'Earl Street'.

An old view of Stanley's builder's yard. George Ruffle painting the handcart.

F. Tippen and Sons ran a haulage firm which carried fruit to market in the 1920s and 1930s. Herbert Tippen (son) stands on the left. The load is of interest showing bushel baskets, ½ bushel baskets, tubs and the New Zealand type BSA box, which was just coming into use. The best fruit still comes from Marden.

Before cars became more generally owned, carriers dealt with many of the out of village requirements. For a small fee the carrier would take a load of rabbits, fruit or any other item, into Maidstone to be sold. Alternatively, anyone in Marden could order something from a Maidstone shop in the morning; this would be sent down to the Carriers' collecting point in the afternoon, and delivered to the purchaser's house the same evening. Frederick Tippen's firm, also, sold cars, motor bikes and carried fruit and vegetables either to the station or straight to the wholesale markets.

In other ways the village had to be self supporting. In the days before the National Health Service it frequently raised money to help maintain the West Kent Hospital as it expanded and it endowed a bed for the use of the village. The advantage of having a nurse to care for people in their own homes was appreciated — but also required the parish to dip into its own pocket.

Marden made a good deal of its own entertainment — football, cricket, dances, concerts, Sunday School and Choir outings, darts, the Flower Show, the W.I. and other societies. The Southern Railway ran a special Derby Day train with saloon coach facilities, which several Marden men enjoyed.

By the outbreak of the war in 1939 Marden was still a village with a strong emphasis on agriculture or agriculture based services. Many men and women worked on farms because high mechanisation had not yet become widespread. Others worked outside the parish, while yet others were unemployed. A few men followed the threshing machines round the district, hoping to be taken on

A haymaking scene at Cornwells Farm in the 1930s.

as the extra help often needed for the job. This lack of work was only relieved by the war.

Most of the children spent all their days at the village school, though a few went to private schools or on to grammar and technical schools at eleven years. The school staff knew the children and their families well.

Although up to 1939 the village was open to newcomers and, as throughout its history, visited, shared events and experiences with other villages and towns, the coming of the war and its aftermath inevitably changed its close-knit character.

Postscript

Marden today has opened up into a different kind of community. The old agricultural domination has gone and, although the actual farms are much the same, the people working on them are a fraction of the pre-war number. Local businesses still thrive and attract trade from outside in many cases, though some shops have disappeared and competition from the large chain stores is an ever present threat. There is a small but busy industrial estate.

Children spend only the first five years of their schooling in Marden and receive all their secondary education outside the parish. Many people, too, work outside either nearby or commuting by train to London.

Marden has acquired a few housing estates since the war and as this process has been gradual absorption of new people into the village has brought few problems and many welcome ideas.

It is, most people think, a lovely place to live.

SOURCES

PRIMARY
West Kent Quarter Sessions Depositions
A Survey of the Parish of Marden 1842
Parish Registers
Vestry Books
Church Wardens' Accounts
Overseers' Accounts
Farm Accounts
Census Returns
Voters' Lists
School Log Books
Parish Council Minutes
Miscellaneous documents in the Kent County Archives
NFU Branch Meeting Minutes
Society for the Protection of Ancient Buildings Archives
Agricultural Returns PRO Kew
House of Commons Select Committee on the South Eastern Railway (House of
    Lords Archives)
Marden, Staplehurst and Collier Street Agricultural Association Minute book

PRINTED
Domesday Monachorum
Domesday Survey
Cal. Pat. Rolls Henry VI Vol. V
Victoria County History
Cal. State Papers (Domestic) 1640-1641 CCCCLXX SP 16
Archbishops' Registers (Canterbury Cath. Archives)
'The History and Topographical Survey of the County of Kent' Edward Hasted
    1797-1801
'A General View of the Agriculture of the County of Kent' John Boys
'Rural Economy of the Southern Counties' (1797) William Marshall
The 'Maidstone Journal'
Parish Magazines

SECONDARY
'History of the Weald of Kent' Edward Furley (1874)
Archaeologia Cantiana Vols. 4, 7, 14, 31, 57, 76
'The Jutish Forest' by K.P. Witney (1976)
'Kent Through the Years' by Christopher Wright (1975)

APPENDIX

List of Marden Vicars (incomplete)

1283	William de Stertinton
1291	John de Sancto Egidio
1321	Robert de Mundeham
	John de Horvyco or Horwilo
1340	Richard de Berham
1352	William de Welde
1367	Henry Stubard
1371/2	John Roo
1373	Lawrence Wympol
1374	William de Wyllaston
1376/7	John de Adyngton
1379	William atte Welde
1381	Roger Stofolde
1397	Thomas Cloker
1412	Peter Gunthorpe
	William Haukyn
1422	Walter Barbour
1423	Thomas Smyth
1425	Nicholas Ledes
1426	John Gay
1434/5	John Thorloke
1443/4	William Reynold
1444	Thomas Therlowe
1446	Michael Courthope
	John Setshire
1458	Baldwin Haukyn
1459	Thomas Cole
1463	John Aston
1467	John Burneham
1475	Thomas Kippok
1477	John Hawkins
1478	John Hewett
1492	John Fleccer
1496/7	John Bradgar

1521/2	Ralph Malleverer
1522/3	Robert Johnson LLB
	John Botyll
1527	John Chamberlyn
1546	John Pogmore
1550	Anthony Burton
1555	Robert Haynes
1562/3	Henry Barnes
1570	Alexander Mascall
1584	Salomon Boxer
1614	John Wood MA

THE COMMONWEALTH:

1644	Gabriel Price
1648	Matthias Sympson
1651/2	Christopher Blackwood
1657	George Amhurst (remaining)

1707	George Fage
1728	William Jacomb
1741	Walter Walker
1748	Jonathon Monckton MA
1766	John Andrews LLB
1811	Frederick Manners-Sutton
1817	Philip le Geyt
1847	Julius Deedes MA
1880	William Benham
1882	Thomas Arnold Carr MA
1906	Robert Edwin-Johnston
1929	John Arthur Finch MA
1952	Cecil George Eagling BA
1965	Hugh Bickersteth Biddell MA
1981	Arthur Cecil Hargreaves MA

INDEX

Vestry, appointment of physician 75; burial ground 77; organisation of 22-25
Vicarage, The Old, illus. 76
Vicars, nineteenth century 75-80

Yalding, Agricultural Riots 43; hops 29; Militia 33; Marden residents born in Yalding 51

Wade, H., illus. 110
Waggon, Kent, illus. 58
Walter, C. 37; S. 38
Wanshurst 37,50
Water supply 92
Watts, W. Churchwarden 25
Watts, W. 73
West End Forge, illus. 111,112,113
West Kent Assize 25

West Kent Regiment of Militia 27,33
Wheat prices 40,43; decline of 45
Wheel plough, Kent illus. 58,59
White Lyon House 19,23, illus. 14
White, R. 82-91; illus. 85
Widehurst Farm 63
Williams, Susan 53
Wilmshurst, John 50
Winchet Hill 53
Winter, Alfred 105
Wolsey, Cardinal 20
Wood, Frank 109
Worcester shim, illus. 70
Workhouse, Marden, see Poorhouse
Wyatt Rebellion, 1554 13
Wye 21

Meresborough Books

Proprietors Hamish and Barbara Mackay Miller
7 STATION ROAD, RAINHAM, GILLINGHAM, KENT. ME8 7RS
Telephone Medway (0634) 388812

We are a specialist publisher of books about Kent. Our books are available in most bookshops in the country, including our own at this address. Alternatively you may order direct, adding 10% for post (minimum 20p, orders over £20.00 post free). ISBN prefix 0 905270 for 3 figure numbers, 094819 for 4 figure numbers. Titles in print July 1986.

BYGONE KENT. A monthly journal on all aspects of Kent history founded October 1979. £1.20 per month. Annual Subscription £13.00. All back numbers available.

HARDBACKS

LIFE AND TIMES OF THE EAST KENT CRITIC: A Kentish Chronicle compiled by **Derrick Molock.** Large format. ISBN 3077. £9.95.

THE PAST GLORY OF MILTON CREEK: Tales of Slipways, Sails and Setting Booms compiled by Alan Cordell and Leslie Williams. ISBN 3042. £9.95.

TALES OF VICTORIAN HEADCORN or The Oddities of Heddington by Penelope Rivers (Ellen M. Poole). ISBN 3050. £8.95. (Also available in paperback ISBN 3069. £3.95.)

ROCHESTER FROM OLD PHOTOGRAPHS compiled by the City of Rochester Society. Large format. ISBN 975. £7.95. (Also available in paperback ISBN 983. £4.95.)

THE LONDON, CHATHAM & DOVER RAILWAY by Adrian Gray. A major study of the development of railways in Kent. ISBN 886. £7.95.

THE NATURAL HISTORY OF ROMNEY MARSH by Dr F.M. Firth, M.A., Ph.D. ISBN 789. £6.95.

O FAMOUS KENT by Eric Swain. The county of Kent in old prints. ISBN 738. £9.95. **BARGAIN OFFER £4.95.**

KENT'S OWN by Robin J. Brooks. The history of 500 (County of Kent) Squadron of the R.A.A.F. ISBN 541. £5.95.

TWO HALVES OF A LIFE by Doctor Kary Pole. The autobiography of a Viennese doctor who escaped from the Nazis and established a new career in Kent. ISBN 509. £5.95.

SOUTH EAST BRITAIN: ETERNAL BATTLEGROUND by Gregory Blaxland. A military history. ISBN 444. £5.95.

HAWKINGE 1912-1961 by Roy Humphreys. A study of the former RAF Station, 100 photographs. ISBN 355. £5.95.

A NEW DICTIONARY OF KENT DIALECT by Alan Major. The first major work on the subject this century. ISBN 274. £7.50.

KENT CASTLES by John Guy. The first comprehensive guide to all the castles and castle sites in Kent. ISBN 150. £7.50.

US BARGEMEN by A.S. Bennett. A new book of sailing barge life around Kent and Essex from the author of 'June of Rochester' and 'Tide Time'. ISBN 207. £6.95.

THE GILLS by Tony Conway. A history of Gillingham Football Club. 96 large format pages packed with old photographs. ISBN 266. £5.95. **BARGAIN OFFER £1.95.**

A VIEW OF CHRIST'S COLLEGE, BLACKHEATH by A.E.O. Crombie, B.A. ISBN 223. £6.95.

JUST OFF THE SWALE by Don Sattin. The story of the barge-building village of Conyer. ISBN 045. £5.95.

TEYNHAM MANOR AND HUNDRED (798-1935) by Elizabeth Selby, MBE. ISBN 630. £5.95.

THE PLACE NAMES OF KENT by Judith Glover. A comprehensive reference work. ISBN 614. £7.50 (also available in paperback. ISBN 622. £3.95)

LARGE FORMAT PICTORIAL PAPERBACKS

OLD PUBS OF TUNBRIDGE WELLS & DISTRICT by Keith Hetherington and Alun Griffiths. A well researched pictorial history with 154 illustrations. ISBN 300X. £3.50.

GOUDHURST: A Pictorial History by John T. Wilson, M.A. ISBN 3026. £2.95.

A PICTORIAL STUDY OF ALKHAM PARISH by Susan Lees and Roy Humphreys. ISBN 3034. £2.95.

THE MOTOR BUS SERVICES OF KENT AND EAST SUSSEX — A brief history by Eric Baldock. An illustrated history from 1899 to 1984 containing 146 photographs. ISBN 959. £4.95.

ROCHESTER FROM OLD PHOTOGRAPHS — see under hardbacks.

PEMBURY IN THE PAST by Mary Standen. ISBN 916. £2.95.

OLD RAMSGATE by Michael David Mirams. ISBN 797. £2.95.

EXPLORING OLD ROCHESTER by John Bryant. A guide to buildings of historic interest. ISBN 827. £2.95.

THOMAS SIDNEY COOPER OF CANTERBURY by Brian Stewart. The life and work of Britain's best cattle painter, with 10 illustrations in colour. ISBN 762. £2.95.

A SECOND PICTUREBOOK OF OLD CHATHAM by Philip MacDougall. ISBN 924. £2.95.

CRANBROOK by Jenni Rodger. A pictorial history. ISBN 746. £2.95.

KENT TOWN CRAFTS by Richard Filmer. A pictorial record of sixteen different crafts. ISBN 584. £2.95.

KENTISH RURAL CRAFTS AND INDUSTRIES by Richard Filmer. A wide variety of rural crafts. ISBN 428. £2.50.

SMARDEN: A PICTORIAL HISTORY by Jenni Rodger. ISBN 592. £2.95.

A PICTUREBOOK OF OLD SHEPPEY by Michael Thomas. 130 Old photographs, mostly from glass negatives. ISBN 657. £2.95.

FIVE MEDWAY VILLAGES by Wyn Bergess and Stephen Sage. A pictorial history of Aylesford, Burham, Wouldham, Eccles and Borstal. ISBN 649. £2.95.

OLD SANDWICH by Julian Arnold and Andrew Aubertin. 146 old photographs. ISBN 673. £2.95.

AVIATION IN KENT by Robin Brooks. A pictorial history from 19th century ballooning to 1939. ISBN 681. £2.95.

A PICTURE BOOK OF OLD RAINHAM by Barbara Mackay Miller. ISBN 606. £2.95.

THE LIFE AND ART OF ONE MAN by Dudley Pout. A Kentish farmer's son who became successful as a commercial artist and as a children's illustrator. ISBN 525. £2.95.

OLD MAIDSTONE'S PUBLIC HOUSES by Irene Hales. 123 photographs. ISBN 533. £2.95.

OLD MAIDSTONE Vol. 1 by Irene Hales and Kay Baldock. ISBN 096. £2.50.

OLD MAIDSTONE Vol. 2 by Irene Hales. ISBN 38X. £2.50.

OLD ASHFORD by Richard Filmer. A photographic study of life in Ashford over 150 years. ISBN 72X. £2.95.

OLD TONBRIDGE by Don Skinner. ISBN 398. £2.50.

KENT TRANSPORT IN OLD POSTCARDS by Eric Baldock. 146 photographs. ISBN 320. £2.95.

GEORGE BARGEBRICK Esq. by Richard-Hugh Perks. The story of Smeed Dean Ltd in Sittingbourne. 80 illustrations. ISBN 479. £2.95.

STANDARD SIZE PAPERBACKS

EXPLORING SUSSEX CHURCHES by John E. Vigar. A companion to 'Exploring Kent Churches'. ISBN 3093. £3.95.

A WEALDEN VILLAGE: MARDEN by Phyllis Highwood and Peggy Skelton. A well researched book for all interested in Wealden history. ISBN 3107. £4.95.

EXPLORING KENT CHURCHES by John E. Vigar. What to look for when visiting a church. ISBN 3018. £3.95.

FLIGHT IN KENT. Another selection of articles by members of the Kent Aviation Historical Research Society. ISBN 3085. £1.95.

TALES OF VICTORIAN HEADCORN — see under hardbacks.

BIRDWATCHING IN KENT by Don Taylor. Details of when and where to watch for which birds, plus very readable accounts of personal experiences. ISBN 932. £4.50.

CRIME AND CRIMINALS IN VICTORIAN KENT by Adrian Gray. An insight into an intriguing if unsavoury side of Victorian life in Kent. ISBN 967. £3.95.

CHIDDINGSTONE — AN HISTORICAL EXPLORATION by Jill Newton. ISBN 940. £1.95.

STOUR VALLEY WALKS from Canterbury to Sandwich by Christopher Donaldson. Enjoy six days walking along the route taken by Caesar, Hengist & Horsa, St Augustine and many others. ISBN 991. £1.95.

THE GHOSTS OF KENT by Peter Underwood, President of the Ghost Club. ISBN 86X. £3.95.

CURIOUS KENT by John Vigar. A selection of the more unusual aspects of Kent history. ISBN 878. £1.95.

REAL ALE PUBS IN KENT by CAMRA in Kent. ISBN 894. £1.50.

A CHRONOLOGY OF ROCHESTER by Brenda Purle. ISBN 851. £1.50.

SITTINGBOURNE & KEMSLEY LIGHT RAILWAY STOCKBOOK AND GUIDE. ISBN 843. 95p.

DOVER REMEMBERED by Jessie Elizabeth Vine. Personal memories from the early years of this century. ISBN 819. £3.95.

THE PLACE NAMES OF KENT — see under hardbacks.

PENINSULA ROUND (The Hoo Peninsula) by Des Worsdale. ISBN 568. £1.50.

A HISTORY OF CHATHAM GRAMMAR SCHOOL FOR GIRLS, 1907-1982 by Audrey Perkyns. ISBN 576. £1.95.

CYCLE TOURS OF KENT by John Guy. No. 1: Medway, Gravesend, Sittingbourne and Sheppey. ISBN 517. £1.50.

ROCHESTER'S HERITAGE TRAIL. (Published for The City of Rochester Society.) A useful guide for the visitor to most places of interest in Rochester. ISBN 169. £1.25.

WINGS OVER KENT. A selection of articles by members of the Kent Aviation Historical Research Society. ISBN 69X. £1.95.

LULLINGSTONE PARK: THE EVOLUTION OF A MEDIAEVAL DEER PARK by Susan Pittman. ISBN 703. £3.95.

LET'S EXPLORE THE RIVER DARENT by Frederick Wood. Walking from Westerham to Dartford. ISBN 770. £1.95.

SAINT ANDREW'S CHURCH, DEAL by Gregory Holyoake. ISBN 835. 95p.

BIRDS OF KENT: A Review of their Status and Distribution. A reprint, with addendum, of the 448 page study by the Kent Ornithological Society. ISBN 800. £6.95.

Further titles are in preparation. Details will be announced in 'Bygone Kent'.